Cordon Bleu

Cheese and Savouries

Cordon Bleu

Cheese and Savouries

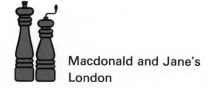

Macdonald and Jane's
London

Published by
Macdonald and Jane's Publishers Ltd
Paulton House
8 Shepherdess Walk
London N1

Copyright B.P.C. Publishing Ltd., 1972

This impression 1977

Designed by Melvin Kyte
Printed by Waterlow (Dunstable) Ltd

These recipes have been adapted from the Cordon Bleu Cookery Course
published by Purnell in association with the London Cordon Bleu
Cookery School
Principal : Rosemary Hume ; Co-Principal : Muriel Downes
Quantities given are for 4 servings.
Spoon measures are level unless otherwise stated.

Contents

Introduction

It has been said that cheese is to milk what wine is to grape juice. Cheese is the best of the milk, the curd, separated from the whey and ripened. The result is a food that is conveniently portable, keeps well, is highly nutritive and, most important of all, is gastronomically far, far more exciting than the original material.

A small portion of cheese is an ideal finish to a good meal, and a well presented cheese board looks most attractive as well. But although cheese is a good and tasty food to eat raw, it is also a useful source of protein to include in cooked meals. For a quick, tasty supper dish or a savoury party snack, cheese is the ideal ingredient. But don't forget there are possibilities as well when you're entertaining; and for something really unusual try one of our sweet cheese dishes.

The recipes included in this . book are of two types — those in which the cheese is the chief ingredient, and those in which a small quantity of cheese is used as a minor, but essential, ingredient. There are dishes, for instance, in which the whole character of the dish is governed by a small sprinkling of cheese added at the last moment, or in which a mere 2 oz cheese in a large savoury mixture regulates both flavour and texture of the finished dish. We make no apology for including these recipes; knowing how to use basic ingredients to give character to a dish is part of a Cordon Bleu cook's skill, and part of the fun of cooking.

There are one or two basic tips to remember before you start. First, never cook cheese for longer than you can help. Overheating makes it tough and indigestible, so if you're making a cheese sauce or a Welsh rarebit, heat the cheese very gently and cook it just long enough to melt it, no more. Second, use a fine grater for a dry cheese or it will be very difficult to melt. A soft cheese should be shredded rather than grated, and very soft cheese can be sliced and added to a sauce without first being grated. Finally, when cheese is very fresh, grate it directly over the dish. Do not sprinkle it with your fingers.

Remember these tips and you're well on the way to successful cheese cookery.

Rosemary Hume
Muriel Downes

Types of cheese

The variety of cheese is almost infinite. The first factor which affects flavour is the type of milk — whether it be cow's, ewe's or goat's, as is usual in Europe, or camel's, llama's, mare's or that of some other milk producing animal. Then climate, vegetation and the method of production all have their effect. The type of soil in an area can affect the flavour of a cheese to such an extent that it cannot be imitated elsewhere — Roquefort is an example where the land which the sheep graze, the limestone caverns where the cheese is matured and the presence of underground lakes in the caverns produce a highly characteristic local cheese. In others, such as Cheddar, the local factor is less significant than the method of manufacture and the cheese can therefore be imitated in all parts of the country and in other parts of the world. The cheese is not less good because of this, but it loses its rarity value.

The separation of curds and whey remains the basis of all cheese production but commercially made cheeses are not now normally allowed to separate naturally. Instead, a small proportion of rennet is added to the warmed, soured milk to accelerate separation. The curd is cooled and salted, often pressed to extract more whey, and left to mature. The degree of treatment varies with the texture of cheese required. If you have access to a supply of unpasteurised milk, you can make a simple curd cheese at home — details are on page 11.

Described below are some of the characteristics of the more common cheeses.

Bel Paese Italian. A rich, creamy cheese with a mild flavour.
Blue Dorset (Blue Vinny) English. A hard, strong-tasting cheese with pronounced blue veining. Texture is stiff and crumbly.
Brie French. A soft, mould inoculated cheese characteristically made in a flat round about 14 inches across. Becomes very soft, almost runny, when mature.
Caerphilly Originally Welsh, but now made in the West of England. A white cheese with a mild,

slightly salty taste and a smooth texture. Eaten very young.

Camembert French. A soft, full cream cheese inoculated with a special white mould which causes fermentation. The cheese is at its best before flavour and smell become too strong. Made in small rounds, 4-5 inches across.

Cheddar English (also Canadian, Irish, New Zealand). Factory produced Cheddar is made in bulk whenever milk is cheap, which makes it an economical buy. Farmhouse Cheddar is made by individual specialists from the milk of a particular herd, a more selective process which is inevitably more expensive. A hard, pale yellow cheese, varying in flavour from mild to fairly strong depending on maturity.

Cheshire English. A hard cheese, either white, red or blue veined. The red is the mildest, but if it ripens to blue it becomes very rich. White Cheshire remains between the two.

Cottage cheese English. One of the few soft cheeses made from skimmed milk. Very white in colour and mild in flavour.

Danish blue A semi-hard, creamy textured cheese ripened with a blue-green mould.

Demi-Sel French. A small, soft cheese, usually weighing about 4 oz. Contains about 2 per cent salt.

Derby English. A hard, white, smooth textured cheese. When young the flavour is mild, but it strengthens as the cheese matures. Layers of finely chopped sage leaves are sometimes added to give **Sage Derby.**

Double Gloucester English. A hard, dark coloured, full flavoured cheese.

Dunlop Included because it is the only Scottish cheese of any note. Similar in flavour to Cheddar but closer in texture and more moist.

Edam Dutch. A semi-hard, mild flavoured cheese. Dark yellow or orange in colour, those exported have a bright red skin.

Emmenthal Swiss (also French, German, Italian). A hard, pale yellow cheese, honeycombed with irregularly placed holes, some of which may be quite large. Springy textured with a mild, sweetish flavour.

Gorgonzola Italian. A semi-hard, blue veined cheese with a very high fat content, at its best when well matured. There is also an excellent white Gorgonzola, but it is rarely available outside Italy.

Gouda Dutch. A semi-hard, mild flavoured cheese similar to Edam, but the best Gouda has a higher fat content.

Gruyère Swiss (also French). A hard, well flavoured cheese, honeycombed with small, regularly placed holes. Emmenthal is often sold under a Gruyère label.

Lancashire English. A hard, crumbly, light coloured cheese excellent for toasting. Flavour is mild.

Leicester English. A hard, red cheese with a crumbly texture. Mild flavoured, sharpening with maturity.

Limburger Belgian (also German). A semi-hard, fermented cheese with a strong smell and a full flavour.

Mozzarella Italian. A semi-soft cheese made from buffalo's milk, though some is now made from cow's milk as well. Eaten young and often used in cooking.

Parmesan Italian. A very hard, pale yellow cheese left to mature for 2-3 years before eating. Strong flavoured, it is best grated and gives a good flavour in cooking.

Petit Suisse French. An unsalted cream cheese made in small cylindrical shapes.

Port Salut French. A semi-hard, fermented cheese with a mild flavour. Originally made by Trappist monks.

Roquefort French. A ewe's milk cheese layered with a culture of mouldy breadcrumbs and matured under highly critical conditions. It is a white, curd-like cheese mottled with blue veins and has a sharp, peppery taste.

Stilton English. A semi-hard cheese, creamy white with blue veins produced from a culture of the same strain as that used in Roquefort. It is rich in cream and strong flavoured.

Wensleydale English. A white, semi-hard cheese that in fact is soft enough to spread. It has a light, almost sweet, flavour. Blue Wensleydale is also made.

Making your own curd cheese

Curd cheese is not frequently made today, at least in urban areas, owing partly to the introduction of pasteurised milk. In the interests of the health of the community, especially in crowded cities, pasteurisation is without doubt a good thing; however, it makes curd cheese-making impossible because the bacteria which cause the natural souring of the milk are destroyed in the pasteurisation process (pasteurised milk which has gone 'off' should be discarded).

Non-pasteurised milk is obtainable in country areas, and when this sours it is not harmful to health, but very good. By law, of course, all milk sold, whether pasteurised or not, is from tuberculin tested cows. Make curd when there is plenty of non-pasteurised milk available as the yield of solid curd from 1 quart of milk is about 4 oz, depending on the quality of the milk.

In warm weather (or at a warm temperature) milk sours more quickly. This is desirable, as the quicker it sours the less likely it is that the resulting curd or cheese will be bitter or over-sour in flavour. If the weather is cold, put the bowl of milk on a shelf in a cupboard in a warm kitchen, or even in an airing cupboard. Leave the milk until it has 'jelled'. This can take up to 2 days (3-4 days is the maximum), but in warm weather, or if a 'starter' has been used, it may jell overnight.

'Starters' hasten the jelling process. A cup of sour milk is the best starter, or use 1 tablespoon or more of yoghourt, depending on the quantity of milk.

Turn the jelled milk into a piece of butter muslin and tie up to form a bag. Hang it up to drip for 12 hours; if the curd is rather soft, leave for a further 6-8 hours. The curd should be nicely firm but not too dry and crumbly.

Untie the muslin and scrape out the curd. Keep in a covered bowl until wanted, then either sieve or beat to remove any small lumps. Season with salt to taste.

Uses of curd

There are several ways of using this curd without further cooking. Beaten up with pepper and salt and a little sour or fresh cream, it becomes the Scots 'crowdie' and is excellent eaten with oatcakes.

With sugar to sweeten well, and as much double cream as you can spare beaten in (up to half the weight of the curd), it becomes the French 'cremets'. This is a delicious accompaniment for cooked fruit in any form.

A little fresh double cream, plain or lightly whipped, may be mixed into the curd and the whole put into small wicker baskets lined with muslin. The curd is then left to drain for about 12 hours before turning out. This is sometimes served with fresh cream poured over it to accompany strawberries or other fruits. When baskets are heart-shaped the cheeses are called 'coeurs à la crème'.

Supper snacks

Give them a tasty surprise for supper with a cooked cheese dish. Whether you are making a meal for family or guests, cheese can be turned into a treat that everybody will enjoy. And don't forget that it provides ample protein for a growing family, much more cheaply than meat or fish.

The first three recipes in this section, the soups, are good for a quick welcome home after a cold evening out, or as a splendid starter to a full meal. The classic French onion soup is a luxury by any standards. Serve one of the more substantial pasta or fish dishes and you will satisfy the healthiest appetites.

One of our favourites is the delicious cheese soufflé on page 24. A soufflé is supposed to be the test of a good cook. In fact it's much more a test of the diners' punctuality, so why not cook it on one of those occasions when the family are all standing round the kitchen waiting for you to produce something good out of nothing? Served straight from the oven on to hot plates it will look and taste a perfect dream.

The most important recipe in cheese cookery is a good, basic mornay sauce. We give the recipe for this here, for you to use in different dishes throughout the book.

Mornay (cheese) sauce

1-1½ oz (2-3 rounded tablespoons) grated cheese
½ teaspoon made mustard (French, or English)
½ pint well-seasoned white, or béchamel, sauce

The cheese may be a mixture of Gruyère and Parmesan or a dry Cheddar. If using Gruyère, which thickens the sauce, reduce the basic roux to ½ oz each butter and flour. If too thick, add a little extra milk.

Method
Make the white or béchamel sauce, remove from heat and gradually stir in grated cheese. When well mixed, add mustard. Reheat but do not boil.

13

Potage crème de fromage

(Cream of cheese soup)

1 large Spanish onion (finely
   chopped)
1½-2 oz butter
2 oz flour
1¾ pints milk (flavoured as for
   use in béchamel sauce)
salt and pepper
pinch of cayenne pepper, or a
   dash of Tabasco sauce
2 egg yolks
2½ fl oz double cream
1½-2 oz Cheshire cheese (finely
   grated)
2-3 tablespoons cooked peas

Method

Put the onion into a pan, cover with cold water and bring to the boil, then drain, rinse and drain again. Melt 1 oz of the butter in a pan, add the onion, cover and cook slowly for about 5 minutes without allowing to colour. Draw aside. Add the rest of the butter, then stir in the flour. The mixture should be soft and fairly liquid.

Blend in the flavoured milk, season with salt, pepper and cayenne (or Tabasco) and stir until boiling. Simmer for 6-7 minutes, or until delicately flavoured, and strain through a fine strainer. Return soup to the rinsed-out pan. Put the egg yolks into a basin, mix with the cream and gradually stir this into the soup, also adding the grated cheese. Reheat carefully, stirring all the time, until thoroughly hot, but do not boil.

Serve this soup with 2-3 tablespoons cooked peas stirred in, and hand a dish of potato croûtons, or cheese profiteroles, separately.

The cheese soup is shown here already garnished with cheese profiteroles (to which guests would normally help themselves)

Stracciatella

1½ pints strong, well-flavoured
    chicken stock (free from
    grease)
3 small eggs
2 oz grated Parmesan cheese
2 tablespoons fine semolina
salt and pepper

This is a Roman speciality, a
garnish which is added to a
good broth.

Method

Put the stock into a pan and
bring to the boil. Break the eggs
into a bowl, beat well with a
fork and add the cheese and
semolina. Add it to 2 tablespoons of the boiling stock,
then pour the mixture into the
remainder of the boiling soup;
whisk vigorously. Boil for one
minute before serving.

Cheese croûtes

Any leftover cream sauce,
cheese or onion, makes a good
croûte. Toast bread on one side,
spread the untoasted side with
sauce and sprinkle well with
grated cheese. Brown well
under the grill. Cut in half and
then into strips. Serve hot
separately with soup.

French onion soup
(Soupe à l'oignon)

5 onions
2 oz butter
2½ pints good bouillon
salt and pepper
1-2 glasses Champagne
    (optional)
3 oz each of Gruyère and
    Parmesan cheese (grated)
1 slice of French bread per
    person
1 egg per person (for serving)

This is perhaps the most famous
of all French soups. This quantity serves 6-8.

Method

Have ready small earthenware
soup pots with lids (*marmites*).
Slice or chop the onions finely
and colour them to a golden-
brown in butter in a frying pan.
Bring the bouillon to the boil
and add the onions; season,
simmer for 5 minutes, then add
the Champagne, if using it.

Mix the cheeses together and
sprinkle a little on the slices of
bread, put a slice into each
marmite, then pour on the
boiling soup. Put on the lids
and serve. Alongside each place
have a small dish of the remaining cheese and a fresh egg.
Each guest breaks the raw egg
into the soup, adds the cheese
and beats it up with a fork. The
soup must be really boiling so
that the egg cooks a little and
thickens the broth slightly.

Macaroni cheese

6 oz macaroni
grated cheese (for topping)
½ pint mornay sauce
extra milk (optional)

A creamy mornay sauce goes especially well with the larger pasta, such as macaroni, which can be served just mixed with the sauce, or gratiné, ie. tipped into a gratin dish and browned to a crisp golden crust in the oven at 425°F or Mark 7.

Method

Break macaroni in half and lower into plenty of boiling salted water. Stir once with a wooden fork or spoon. Simmer until tender (about 20 minutes, macaroni should be cooked a little more than spaghetti), then drain in a colander. Pour over 1-2 cups of hot water, drain again well, then tip back into the saucepan, cover and keep warm while making the sauce.

Prepare mornay sauce and season well. Add sauce to the macaroni, stir gently to mix, then turn into a gratin dish. Grate cheese on top to cover fairly thickly then brown in the oven at 425°F or Mark 7 for about 15 minutes.

Watchpoint For a good macaroni cheese there must be ample sauce — add a little extra milk if sauce is too thick after the addition of the cheese.

Tomato and macaroni cheese

1 medium-size can (14 oz)
  tomatoes
8 oz cut macaroni
salt
pepper (ground from mill)
1 oz butter
4-6 oz grated Cheddar cheese

Many grocers sell Cheddar cheese ready-grated, so buying this will save you time.

Method

Cook the macaroni as directed on the packet, then drain well and reserve. Lift tomatoes out of the can with a draining spoon and season them well.

Cover the bottom of a buttered ovenproof dish with a layer of grated cheese and then a layer of seasoned tomatoes. Arrange the macaroni on top and cover with a further layer of tomatoes and the remainder of the cheese. Bake in the oven, pre-set at 375°F or Mark 5, for about 20-30 minutes or until brown and crisp on top.

Cheese and tomato rice

1 oz grated Cheddar cheese
1 oz grated Parmesan cheese
½ pint strong tomato pulp
2 cups freshly boiled long grain rice
1 oz butter
1 clove of garlic (crushed)
1 onion (chopped)
salt and pepper

Method

Heat the butter and sauté the garlic and onion until soft, add the rice and tomatoes, season well and heat thoroughly. Add the cheese just before serving.

Cheese, cauliflower and mushroom strudel

2 oz dry grated cheese
1 cauliflower
2 oz mushrooms (sliced and cooked)
2 tablespoons fresh white
   breadcrumbs
1 dessertspoon chopped parsley
salt and pepper
paprika pepper
strudel dough (see page 100)
½ pint mornay sauce (for serving)

Method

Break the cauliflower into sprigs and cook until just tender. Drain well and mix with remaining ingredients. Roll out the strudel dough, spread with the filling and bake the strudel as for cream cheese strudel 1 (but omit dusting with sugar). Serve with mornay sauce.

Cheese and smoked haddock strudel

2 oz grated cheese
1 lb smoked haddock
1-2 hard-boiled eggs (chopped)
6 tablespoons fresh white
   breadcrumbs
salt and pepper
chopped chives
strudel dough (see page 100)
½ pint mornay sauce (for serving)

Method

Poach the haddock in water until tender, bone and flake and put into a bowl with the cheese, eggs, breadcrumbs and seasoning. Roll out the strudel dough, spread with the filling, and bake as for cream cheese strudel 1. Serve the sauce separately.

Cheese fondue soufflé

¾ pint milk
1 oz butter
1½ teaspoons salt
pepper (ground from mill)
pinch of cayenne pepper
6 oz fresh white breadcrumbs
4 oz grated Gruyère cheese
1 clove of garlic (crushed
    with a little salt)
4 eggs (separated)

Method

Set the oven at 375°F or Mark 5. Bring the milk to the boil, then stir in the butter, salt and peppers, and pour the mixture over the breadcrumbs. Add the garlic and cheese, return mixture to the pan and stir over moderate heat until cheese melts. Beat in the egg yolks. Cool the mixture slightly, then stiffly whip the egg whites and fold them into the mixture. Pour into a buttered pie dish (it should not be more than three-quarters full), and bake in the pre-set oven for about 40 minutes.

Toasted cheese 1

4-6 oz Leigh, or dry Cheddar, cheese (thinly sliced)
little made mustard
pepper
2-3 tablespoons brown ale
hot, dry toast

Method

Slice cheese thinly into the dish or pan in which you will be serving it at the table. Spread over the mustard and add plenty of pepper.

Pour over the ale, cover and set dish in a bain-marie on low heat until beginning to melt. Remove from heat, stir carefully then put back on heat until it is all melted.

Serve at once, with hot dry toast handed separately.

Toasted cheese 2

3 oz grated Cheddar cheese
1½ oz butter
1-2 tablespoons boiling milk
salt and pepper
cayenne pepper
slices of toast
anchovy paste (optional)

Method

Work the cheese and butter together, and add the milk gradually until of a creamy consistency; season to taste. Spread the toast with anchovy paste if wished, and then with the cheese mixture. Arrange in a shallow flameproof dish and brown under a hot grill. Serve immediately.

Ramekins au fromage (cheese ramekins)

2 eggs
2 oz Cheddar cheese (grated)
seasoning
½ pint milk
2 slices stale bread (for
   croûtons)
butter (for frying)
8 anchovy fillets
paprika pepper (for dusting)

*6-8 ramekins, or individual soufflé
   dishes*

Method

Set oven at 375°F or Mark 5. Beat the eggs, add the cheese, seasoning and milk. Cut and fry the croûtons. Divide each anchovy fillet into 2-3 pieces. Butter the dishes, put a spoonful of the croûtons and some pieces of anchovy in each one and fill with the egg mixture.

Cook au bain-marie in pre-set oven until golden-brown and firm to the touch (about 15-20 minutes). Dust with paprika pepper and serve.

Welsh rarebit

4 oz Leigh, or well matured
   Cheddar, cheese (grated)
¾ oz butter
2 tablespoons brown ale, or milk
1 teaspoon made mustard
cayenne pepper
squares of hot buttered toast

Method

Melt butter in a shallow pan, put in the cheese and melt it slowly by standing in a bain-marie on top of the stove. Be careful not to get it too hot. Gradually stir in the ale or milk and seasonings. When creamy, turn on to the hot buttered toast and serve at once.

Golden buck

4 oz Cheddar cheese (grated)
2½ fl oz brown ale
1 oz butter
pinch of celery salt
pinch of paprika pepper
pepper (ground from mill)
2 eggs (beaten)
1 tablespoon cream
½ teaspoon Worcestershire sauce
4 rounds freshly made toast (crusts
   removed)

Method

Put the cheese, ale, butter, salt and peppers into a pan and place over gentle heat. When the cheese begins to melt add the eggs and cream. Stir over heat until thick and creamy; add the Worcestershire sauce. Arrange the toast on a hot serving dish, and pour over the mixture.

Cheese cream

6 oz mixed cheeses (free from
   rind), or use Cheddar, or
   Cheshire, alone
3 oz butter, or luxury margarine
1 teacup hot milk
mixed herbs (chopped), or chives
   (snipped) — optional
salt and pepper

Method

Grate cheese. Cream butter well in a basin, then work in cheese gradually. When mixture becomes stiff, add hot milk and continue beating until it is light and creamy.

Add herbs and/or chives to taste, or leave plain. Season well with salt and plenty of pepper. Serve with toast or as a sandwich filling.

Luncheon cheese

4 oz strongly flavoured cheese
   (eg. Danish Blue)
2 oz butter
1 heart of celery (chopped),
   or a pinch of celery salt
¾ oz shallots (grated)
1 tablespoon chopped parsley
salt
pepper (ground from mill)
little cream (optional)
3-4 tablespoons chopped
   cashews, walnuts, or almonds

Method

Sieve the cheese and beat well with 1 oz of the butter. Add the celery, shallot, and seasoning, and add the cream if needed to make the mixture light and creamy. Press the mixture into a pat. Brown the nuts lightly in the remaining butter, toss in salt and cover the cheese with them before serving.

Roquefort mousse

4 oz Roquefort cheese
½ oz gelatine
3 tablespoons lemon juice
6 fl oz hot water
1 cup grated cucumber (drained)
3 tablespoons chopped parsley
2 tablespoons chopped pimiento
1 teaspoon chopped onion
1 teaspoon salt
black pepper
7½ fl oz double cream (lightly
    whipped)
watercress (to garnish)

7-inch diameter ring mould

Method
Soften gelatine in lemon juice,
add hot water to dissolve.
Crush cheese and mix with
cucumber, parsley, pimiento and
onion. Add seasoning and stir.
Stir in gelatine, stand bowl on
ice to thicken and fold in the
cream. Pour into the mould and
chill until firm. Turn out and fill
centre with watercress.

Gannat

½ lb plain flour (sifted with 2 pinches
    of salt and 1 of pepper)
1 teaspoon sugar
½ oz yeast
4 fl oz milk
2 oz butter, or luxury margarine
2 eggs
4 oz Gruyère, or Emmenthal, or
    Cheshire, cheese (grated)

*Deep 7-inch diameter sandwich tin,
or 1lb loaf tin*

This is a rich cheese bread
which makes delicious sandwiches or can be used as a
bread and butter accompaniment to a first course.

Method
Place flour in a warm bowl and
make a well in the centre.
Cream sugar with yeast and
place in the well of flour.
  Warm the milk with the butter
in a pan; when dissolved and the
mixture is only lukewarm, stir
into the flour with the eggs, well
beaten to a froth.
  Work well to form a soft
dough, cover and leave to stand
until double in bulk (45 minutes
to 1 hour). Then work in the
cheese, reserving 1 tablespoon.
  Set oven at 400°F or Mark 6.
  Turn mixture into the greased
tin. Leave to prove, sprinkle with
rest of cheese and bake in pre-
set oven for about 45-50
minutes, until a good brown.
Serve hot or cold.
  If baked in a sandwich tin, it
may be split and sandwiched
with cheese cream (see left).

Cheese omelet

4 eggs
1½ tablespoons cold water
salt
black pepper (ground from mill)
1 oz butter
2-3 tablespoons grated
    Cheddar, or Gruyère, cheese

7-8 inch diameter omelet pan

This quantity serves 2. For more people it is better to make another omelet than to increase the size.

Method

Break eggs into a basin and beat well with a fork. When well mixed, add water and seasoning (this should be done just before making it). Heat pan on medium heat. Put in butter in two pieces and, when frothing, pour in egg mixture at once. Leave 10-15 seconds before stirring round slowly with the flat of a fork. Do this once or twice round pan, stop and leave for another 5-6 seconds.

Lift up edge of omelet to let any remaining raw egg run on to hot pan. Scatter the cheese thickly over the omelet. Now tilt pan away from you and fold over omelet to far side. Change your grip on pan so that the handle runs up the palm of your hand. Take the hot dish or plate in your other hand, tilt it slightly and tip omelet on to it. Serve at once.

Cheese soufflé

4 rounded tablespoons grated
    cheese (Parmesan and Gruyère)
1½ oz butter
1 rounded tablespoon plain flour
salt
cayenne pepper
¾ cup milk
1 teaspoon ready-made mustard
4 egg yolks
5 egg whites
1 tablespoon browned crumbs

*7-inch diameter top (size No. 1)
    soufflé dish*

Method

Rub the inside of the soufflé dish lightly with butter and dust with crumbs. Tie a band of greaseproof paper round the outside of the dish, to stand about 3 inches above the rim; butter the paper. Set oven at 375°F or Mark 5.

Make a roux by melting the butter, removing pan from heat and stirring in the flour. Season well, blend in milk. Put pan back on heat, stir until boiling then draw aside. Add mustard and beat in 3 rounded tablespoons cheese and egg yolks one at a time.

When well mixed whip egg whites to a firm snow, stir 2 tablespoons of the whites into the sauce, using a metal spoon. Then stir in the remainder in two parts, lifting the sauce well over the whites from the bottom of the pan. Turn the bowl round while mixing; do not overmix.

Turn lightly into prepared soufflé dish. Quickly dust top with crumbs and rest of cheese mixed together. Bake for 25-30 minutes in pre-set oven, until evenly brown and firm to the touch. Serve immediately.

Cold cheese soufflé

½ pint béchamel sauce
2 egg yolks
3 oz dry cheese (grated, with a
   little Parmesan added)
salt and pepper
1 teaspoon French mustard
¾ oz gelatine
⅛ pint stock, or water
squeeze of lemon juice
4 fl oz double cream (lightly
   whipped)
3 egg whites (stiffly whipped)

For garnish
bunch of watercress
2-3 tomatoes (sliced)
Parmesan cheese (grated)

*6-inch diameter top (size No. 2)
   soufflé dish*

Method
Tie a band of greaseproof paper
round the outside of the soufflé
dish, oil dish and paper above
edge of dish and stand an oiled
jam jar in the middle.

Make the béchamel sauce,
cool slightly, then beat in the
egg yolks, cheese and seasonings. Dissolve the gelatine in
stock or water, add to the
mixture with the lemon juice.
When quite cold, fold in the
cream, lightly whipped, and
lastly the stiffly whipped egg
whites.

Turn the mixture into prepared
dish and leave to set. Carefully remove jar and paper and
fill centre with watercress.
Garnish the top with sliced
tomatoes and press Parmesan
cheese round the sides.

Watchpoint The cheese for
the soufflé itself must be dry
and full of flavour with a little
Parmesan added, otherwise it
will be too bland.

Individual cold cheese soufflés

3 oz Parmesan cheese (grated)
2 oz Gruyère cheese (grated)
salt and pepper
pinch of cayenne pepper
½ teaspoon French mustard
½ pint good aspic jelly (cool,
   but not set)
2 teaspoons tarragon vinegar
¾ pint double cream
browned breadcrumbs
olives — to serve

6-8 individual soufflé dishes

Method
Oil the soufflé dishes and tie
a piece of greaseproof paper
around the outsides, to come
above the rims of the dishes.

Put the grated cheese and
seasonings in a bowl and mix
well together. Add the aspic
and vinegar. Stiffly whip the
cream and fold it into the
mixture. Fill it into the soufflé
dishes, so that the mixture
comes above the rims. Put into
the refrigerator to set, then
remove the paper, dust with the
crumbs and decorate with olives.

(To remove the stones from
green olives without spoiling
their shape, make a small cut
across the top of the olive with
a sharp knife. Then, keeping the
blade of the knife against the
stone, work in a spiral removing
the flesh until you get to the
base of the stone. Then remove
the flesh from the bottom and
reshape the olive. Black olives,
being soft, can be stoned by slit-
ting down one side and using the
point of a small knife to lever
out the stone.)

Cheese soufflé with sweetcorn

For soufflé mixture
1 cup sweetcorn kernels
 (blanched)
2 tablespoons grated cheese
 (preferably Gruyère and Parmesan mixed)
1½ oz butter
1½ oz plain flour
good ½ pint milk (flavoured as
 for a béchamel)
2-3 tablespoons double cream
cayenne pepper
salt and pepper
4 egg yolks
5 egg whites
grated cheese (for dusting)

For mornay sauce
1¼ oz butter
1 oz plain flour
¾ pint milk
2-3 oz cheese (grated)
salt and pepper

*7-inch diameter top (size No. 1)
 soufflé dish*

Method

Set the oven at 375°F or Mark 5.
Prepare the soufflé dish (see
page 24).

Melt the butter in a large pan,
draw it aside and stir in the
flour. Pour in the milk, blend and
stir until boiling. Draw pan
aside, beat in the cream, the
well-drained corn, seasoning,
cheese and the yolks, one at a
time.

Whisk whites stiffly, cut and
fold one large spoonful into the
sauce, then add the remaining
white in two parts. Continue to
cut and fold but be careful not to
overmix (as this expels air).
Turn mixture into soufflé dish,
dust the top with grated cheese,
stand dish on a baking sheet
and set in the centre of pre-set
oven. Bake for 25-35 minutes.

Meanwhile prepare the mornay sauce in the usual way.
When soufflé is cooked, serve
immediately with the mornay
sauce handed separately.

Omelet Arnold Bennett

4 eggs (separated)
4 tablespoons smoked haddock
  (cooked and flaked)
2 oz butter
¼ pint cream
salt and pepper
3 tablespoons grated Parmesan
  cheese

This is an elegant dish which was created for the writer, Arnold Bennett, by the Savoy Grill in London. It is one of the best omelets. Serves 2.

Method

Toss the haddock with 1 oz butter and 2 tablespoons cream in a pan over a quick heat, for about 2-3 minutes, allow to cool.

Beat the egg yolks with 1 tablespoon cream and season. Whip the egg whites lightly, fold into the yolks with the haddock and add half the cheese.

Melt the rest of the butter in the pan and cook omelet. Do not fold, but slide omelet on to a hot dish, sprinkle on rest of cheese and pour the cream over it. Brown quickly under a hot grill and serve at once.

Scrambled eggs with cream cheese

6 eggs
2 small cream cheeses (Gervais
  or Petit Suisse)
4 cream crackers
butter
5-6 tablespoons creamy milk
salt
pepper (ground from mill)
pinch of cayenne pepper
1 teaspoon finely chopped herbs
  (chives, chervil, or basil)

Method

Warm the cream crackers and butter them. Beat the cheese with a fork and soften with a spoonful of milk. Melt the remaining butter, add the milk, seasoning and herbs. Beat the eggs lightly and add to the mixture. Cook over moderate heat, stirring and scraping the mixture from bottom of pan with a spoon to get thick creamy flakes. Just before the eggs 'scramble' add the cheese, taste for seasoning and spoon on to cream crackers to serve immediately.

Eggs en cocotte

4-5 eggs
8-15 small slices of Gruyère
  cheese
salt and pepper
4-5 tablespoons double cream
paprika pepper

4-5 individual cocottes

Method
Half fill a pan with boiling salted water. Butter the cocottes well and put 2-3 small slices of cheese in the bottom of each. Break in the eggs, season and add 1 tablespoon cream to each cocotte. Dust with paprika, stand the cocottes in the water (let water come just up to rims), cover with a lid and cook very slowly for 7-8 minutes until the eggs are just setting.

Eggs florentine

6 new-laid eggs
1½ lb spinach
½ oz butter
salt and pepper

For mornay sauce
1½ oz butter
1¼ oz plain flour
½-¾ pint milk
2 oz Cheddar, or Cheshire,
  cheese (grated)
salt and pepper
little made English mustard

New-laid eggs are best for poaching, otherwise the white will detach itself from the yolk.

Method
Poach the eggs in a saucepan or deep frying pan filled with boiling water — add about 1 tablespoon vinegar to 1 quart water, keep heat low and water gently simmering; break eggs into pan and poach for 3½-4½ minutes until firm. Lift out with a draining spoon and leave in cold water until wanted. Boil the spinach, drain and press. Then return to the pan with ½ oz butter and season. Shake pan over the heat for 1-2 minutes, then arrange spinach down the centre of an ovenproof dish; drain and dry the eggs and place on top.

Prepare the mornay sauce; allow it to boil well, then draw pan aside before adding 1½ oz of the cheese. Season the sauce well and coat the eggs with it. Sprinkle with the rest of cheese and brown under the grill, or in a quick oven at 425°F or Mark 7, for 5-6 minutes.

Eggs Suzette

5 small new-laid eggs
5 large potatoes
salt
4 oz mushrooms (sliced)
1¼ oz butter
1 teaspoon plain flour
2-3 tablespoons stock
4 oz cooked ham (sliced and
   shredded)
2 tablespoons hot milk
grated cheese

For mornay sauce
½ oz butter
½ oz plain flour
¼ pint milk
1 oz cheese (grated)

Method
Clean potatoes, but do not peel,
roll them in salt and bake in
oven at 350°F or Mark 4 for
about 1½ hours or until tender.

Sauté the sliced mushrooms
in about ½ oz butter in a small
pan, then dust with flour.
Moisten with the stock, bring
to the boil, add the ham and set
aside. Make the mornay sauce
and poach or soft-boil the eggs.

Cut off the tops of the
potatoes (lengthways) and
carefully scoop out the pulp.
Put this into a warm basin and
mash thoroughly. Add ½ oz
butter and hot milk to make a
purée.

Put a spoonful of the mushroom and ham mixture into the
bottom of each potato, place a
well-drained egg on top and
coat with the mornay sauce.
Top with the purée of potato, to
cover the eggs completely.
Sprinkle with grated cheese and
brown under grill, or in oven
at 400°F or Mark 6, for 10
minutes. Serve hot.

Eggs à la crème with mushrooms

5-6 eggs
3 oz mushrooms (sliced)
½ oz butter
squeeze of lemon juice
salt and pepper
¼ pint double cream
pinch of grated nutmeg
3 oz Gruyère cheese (grated)

5-6 ramekins

Method
Cook the sliced mushrooms
very quickly in the butter with
a squeeze of lemon. Pour half
the cream into the ramekins,
break the eggs carefully on top
and then cover with the
mushrooms.

Season the remaining cream,
add grated nutmeg, and spoon it
over the mushrooms. Cover
each ramekin with a thick
layer of grated Gruyère cheese,
stand in a bain-marie of very hot
water and cook in oven at
350°F or Mark 4 for 10 minutes.
Serve hot.

Eggs cantalienne

4 large eggs (hard-boiled)
1 small cabbage
2 oz butter
1 wineglass white wine, or stock
salt and pepper
2 shallots (finely chopped)
browned crumbs

For sauce
1 oz butter
1 rounded tablespoon plain flour
½ pint milk
½ teaspoon French mustard
1½ oz cheese (grated)

> **Cantal** is a cheese of the Auvergne district of France, made from a mixture of cow's, ewe's and goat's milk. Grated Cheddar cheese is also suitable for eggs cantalienne.

Method

Cut the cabbage in quarters, remove the hard stalk and shred leaves finely. Blanch in pan of boiling salted water for 1 minute, drain and return to the pan with 1 oz butter and wine or stock. Season, cover with buttered paper and the lid and simmer for 5-6 minutes until the cabbage is just tender.

Meanwhile prepare the sauce: melt 1 oz butter in a pan, add flour and blend in half the milk. Stir until boiling, draw aside and mix in mustard and three-quarters of the cheese.

Cook the chopped shallots slowly in the remaining 1 oz butter until soft.

Split the eggs lengthways. Remove the yolks, rub them through a wire sieve and mix with the shallots and 2 tablespoons sauce. Fill the whites as fully as possible with the mixture. Add the rest of the milk to the sauce and reheat.

Dish up the cabbage and lay down the centre of a hot serving dish, arrange the eggs on top and spoon over the sauce. Sprinkle with browned crumbs mixed with remaining grated cheese and brown under grill, or in oven at 400°F or Mark 6, for 10 minutes.

Quiche lorraine

For rich shortcrust pastry
6 oz plain flour
pinch of salt
3 oz butter, or margarine
1 oz shortening
2 tablespoons cold water

For filling
1 egg
1 egg yolk
1 rounded tablespoon grated
   cheese
salt and pepper
½ pint single cream, or milk
½ oz butter
2-3 rashers of streaky bacon
   (diced)
1 small onion (thinly sliced), or
   12 spring onions

7-inch diameter flan ring

Hot or cold, this cheese, egg and bacon tart is a typical dish from the Lorraine region of France.

Method

Make the rich shortcrust pastry and set aside to chill.

When chilled, line the pastry on to the flan ring. Beat the egg and extra yolk in a bowl, add the cheese, seasoning and cream or milk. Melt the butter in a small pan, add the bacon and sliced onion, or whole spring onions, and cook slowly until just golden in colour. Then turn contents of the pan into the egg mixture, mix well and pour into the pastry case.

Bake for about 25-30 minutes in an oven at 375°F or Mark 5.

Salé

(Swiss cheese dish)

For rich shortcrust pastry
6 oz plain flour
pinch of salt
3 oz butter
1 oz shortening
1 egg yolk
2 tablespoons cold water

For filling
½ pint béchamel sauce
little double cream
3 eggs
4½ oz Gruyère cheese (grated)
salt and pepper
grated nutmeg

7-inch diameter flan ring

Method

Make the rich shortcrust pastry and set aside to chill. When chilled, line the pastry on to the flan ring. Make the béchamel sauce (but add a little cream to it) and when cool beat in the eggs and grated cheese; add plenty of seasoning and a grating of nutmeg. Pour the mixture into the pastry case and bake for about 25 minutes in an oven at 375-400°F or Mark 5-6.

Pissaladière

For rich shortcrust pastry
8 oz plain flour
pinch of salt
4 oz butter
2 oz shortening
1 egg yolk
2 tablespoons cold water

For filling
1 lb onions (thinly sliced)
4 tablespoons olive oil
12-15 black olives (stoned)
2 teaspoons French mustard
6-8 tomatoes (skinned and
   thickly sliced)
14 anchovy fillets (split lengthways, soaked in 2-3 tablespoons milk)
2 oz Gruyère cheese (grated)
mixed herbs (basil, thyme, sage)
   —chopped

7-8 inch diameter flan ring

This flan, with its black olives and anchovy fillets, is characteristic of dishes from Nice in southern France.

Method

Make the rich shortcrust pastry, line on to the flan ring and chill.

Cook the onions slowly in half the oil for about 20 minutes until golden, and then cool. Stone the black olives.

Spread the mustard over the pastry, place the onions evenly on top, then arrange the tomato slices over and cover these with a lattice of anchovy fillets (well drained from the milk), and place a halved olive in each space. Sprinkle a few herbs over the top and finish with the grated cheese. Spoon the remaining oil over flan and bake for about 30-35 minutes in an oven at 400°F or Mark 6.

Tarte au poisson

For rich shortcrust pastry
8 oz plain flour
4 oz butter
1 oz shortening
1 egg yolk
2-3 tablespoons water (to mix)

For filling
7 oz can tunny fish (flaked)
4 tomatoes
1 oz butter
2-3 onions (finely sliced)
½ oz plain flour
¼ pint milk
salt and pepper
grated nutmeg
2 eggs (beaten)
2 oz grated cheese

8-inch diameter flan ring

Less shortening is used than in the previous recipe in order to make the tart less rich.

Method

First prepare the rich shortcrust pastry and chill. Roll out pastry and line into a plain or fluted flan ring and bake blind for about 15 minutes. Meanwhile scald and skin tomatoes, cut in half, remove seeds, and set flesh on one side.

Melt the butter in a pan, add the onions and cook until soft. Mix in the flour and add the milk. Stir sauce until boiling, draw aside and add seasoning, nutmeg, and beaten eggs. Arrange the tomatoes and flaked tunny fish in the bottom of the flan, season, and pour in the sauce to fill well.

Scatter with grated cheese and put into the oven, pre-set at 350°F or Mark 4, until well set and golden-brown (about 30 minutes). Serve warm.

Tomato tart

For rich shortcrust pastry
8 oz plain flour
pinch of salt
4 oz butter
2 oz lard
1 egg yolk
2-3 tablespoons water

For filling
4½ oz fresh breadcrumbs
8 tomatoes
6 oz cheese (Cheddar, or Gruyère)
— grated
¼ pint double cream
1 tablespoon chopped mixed
herbs and parsley
1 dessertspoon anchovy essence
salt and pepper
grate of nutmeg (optional)

8-9 inch diameter flan ring

Method

Make up the pastry and chill well. Line it into the flan ring, making sure that there is a good edge standing up ¼ inch above the ring. Prick the bottom with a fork and set aside to chill. Set the oven at 400°F or Mark 6.

Meanwhile prepare the filling: lightly brown the crumbs in the oven. Scald and skin the tomatoes, cut them in half, remove the stalk and seeds. Sprinkle tomatoes well with salt and leave them to stand for about 30 minutes. Tip off any liquid and dry the halves well.

Scatter the browned crumbs into the bottom of the flan, arrange the tomatoes on top in a single layer, rounded sides uppermost, mix the cheese and cream together with the herbs and anchovy essence. Season well and add a little grating of nutmeg. Spoon this mixture over the tomatoes and bake tart in the pre-set hot oven for 30-40 minutes.

If the tart is browning too quickly after 25 minutes, lower the oven to 350°F or Mark 4 and continue to cook until the pastry shrinks slightly from the flan ring. Then remove the ring, and put the tart back into the oven for a few minutes. Serve hot or cold.

Pizza napolitana

¼ quantity of basic pizza dough

For topping
4-6 anchovy fillets
2 tablespoons milk
1 lb ripe tomatoes
1-2 tablespoons olive oil
1 small onion (finely chopped)
1 dessertspoon chopped
   marjoram, or basil
salt and pepper
4 oz Bel Paese, or Mozzarella,
   cheese (sliced)

8-inch diameter flan ring

Method

Flour the dough lightly and pat it out with the palm of your hand on floured baking sheet to a round 8 inches in diameter. Then place greased flan ring over it.

Split the anchovy fillets in two lengthways and soak them in the milk; set aside.

Scald and skin the tomatoes, cut away the hard core, squeeze gently to remove seeds, then slice. Heat the oil in a frying pan; add chopped onion and, after a few minutes, the sliced tomatoes. Draw pan aside and add the herbs; season well.

Set oven at 400°F or Mark 6.

Cover dough with tomato mixture, place cheese slices on this and arrange anchovies lattice-wise over the top. Prove pizza for 10-15 minutes, then bake in pre-set oven for 30-35 minutes. Lift off flan ring and slide pizza on to a bread board or wooden platter to serve.

Basic pizza dough

1 lb plain flour
1 teaspoon salt
1 oz yeast
2 teaspoons sugar
about ¼ pint milk (warmed)
3-4 eggs (beaten)
4 oz butter (creamed)

Method

Sift the flour and salt into a warmed basin. Cream yeast and sugar and add to the warmed milk with the beaten eggs; add this liquid to the flour and beat thoroughly. Work the creamed butter into the dough. Cover and leave for 40 minutes to rise. **Note:** for the best pizza, it is wise to use a flan ring to keep the dough in position. It has the added advantage of enabling you to cover the entire surface with topping without it running and sticking to your baking sheet.

The name **Pizza** originated from the area around Naples. It is not certain, however, that the nearby village of Pizza, where the flour for the best pizza dough is grown and ground, can claim to be its creator. A pizza may first have been made to use up left-over bread dough and tomato sauce, plus whatever sausage, ham or cheese happened to be available.

Fish Monte Carlo

1 lb white fish, or smoked
   haddock (cooked)
1 can sweetcorn kernels
1 oz butter
1 oz plain flour
½ pint milk
salt and pepper
pinch of mustard
2 eggs (separated)
2 oz cheese (grated)

For serving
4-5 bacon rashers
tomato sauce

Pie dish (1-1½ pints capacity)

Method

Remove the skin and bone from the fish and flake the flesh. Drain sweetcorn, melt butter, add flour and mix. Pour on the milk, stir until boiling, season and add the mustard; draw the pan aside and stir in the corn. Beat in the egg yolks and cheese, reserving a little for the top. Whip egg whites and fold into the sauce.

Butter an ovenproof dish, fill by layering the sauce and fish together, finishing with the sauce. Sprinkle with the remaining cheese and crumbs and bake in a moderate oven at 350°F or Mark 4 for 20-30 minutes.

Before serving, garnish with the bacon, grilled, and serve a tomato sauce separately.

Skate au gratin

2 lb wing of skate
court bouillon, or water plus
  1-2 tablespoons vinegar
about 16 button onions
½ oz butter
1 teaspoon sugar
triangular pieces of bread
  (for croûtes)
oil (for frying)

For sauce
¾ pint milk (infused with 1 slice
  of onion, 1 blade mace, 4-5
  peppercorns, few parsley
  stalks)
1 oz butter
1 rounded tablespoon plain flour
salt and pepper
2 oz cheese (grated)

Court bouillon

Slice 1 large carrot and 1 onion. Place these in a pan with 2 pints of water, bouquet garni, 6 peppercorns, 2 tablespoons vinegar (or juice of ½ lemon). Salt lightly, cover, and simmer for 8-10 minutes. Cool, and strain.

Method

First make court bouillon, then set aside. Cut skate into fingers, put in a shallow pan and cover with court bouillon, or water and vinegar. Simmer for 20 minutes. Draw pan aside.

To prepare sauce: heat and infuse milk and then pour into a jug. Melt butter in the pan used for flavouring milk, stir in flour and cook roux to a pale straw colour. Strain on the milk, blend and stir until boiling. Draw pan aside, adding seasoning and three-quarters of the cheese, a little at a time. Set this aside.

Blanch onions, drain and return to the pan with ½ oz butter and 1 teaspoon sugar. Cover and cook for 5-7 minutes until golden-brown and tender. Shake pan occasionally. Fry bread in oil until brown.

Drain pieces of skate, remove skin and arrange in an ovenproof dish, spoon over the sauce, sprinkle on the remaining cheese and brown in the oven at 425°F or Mark 7 for 7-10 minutes. Serve garnished with the glazed onions and croûtes.

Smoked haddock roulade

8 oz (2 cups) smoked haddock
(cooked and flaked)
4 eggs
3 rounded tablespoons grated
dry cheese

For filling
béchamel sauce made with 1½ oz
butter, 2½ tablespoons flour,
¾ pint flavoured, or plain, milk
salt and pepper
1 dessertspoon anchovy essence
3 eggs (hard-boiled and finely
chopped)

*Swiss roll tin (12 inches by 8 inches),
or baking sheet with a raised edge*

Tunny fish, canned or fresh salmon or crab meat may be used in this dish instead of haddock.

Method

First prepare the filling: make béchamel sauce, season and add anchovy essence. The sauce should be creamy and thick enough just to drop from the spoon.

Take 3 tablespoons of sauce and add to the cooked fish. Add the chopped eggs to the remaining sauce; cover and set aside but keep warm.

Grease tin or baking sheet well. Line with greaseproof paper and grease again. Set oven at 400°F or Mark 6.

Separate eggs and beat yolks into the fish with one-third of the cheese. Whip whites to a firm snow and cut and fold into fish mixture with a metal spoon.

Put on to the tin and spread evenly. Bake on top shelf of

Smoked haddock roulade: prepare fish, filling and sauce, mix a little sauce with fish and beat in yolks and cheese

Having stirred egg whites into fish mixture, spread evenly over the case set on a greased baking sheet. Bake in the oven until firm

Smoked haddock roulade continued

pre-set oven for 10-15 minutes or until well risen and firm to the touch.

Have ready a large sheet of greaseproof paper, sprinkled with the remaining cheese. Quickly turn the roulade on to this, strip off the paper it was cooked on and spread roulade with the filling. Trim off sides, then tilt paper and roll up mixture in the same way as for a swiss roll. Put on to a hot serving dish and sprinkle with additional cheese, if wished.

Turn cooked roulade on to greaseproof paper sprinkled with cheese; spread filling over roulade, trim sides, tilt paper and roll up

Fillets of haddock florentine

1-1½ lb haddock fillet (skinned)
salt
lemon juice
1 lb leaf spinach
½ oz butter

For mornay sauce
¾ oz butter
1 rounded tablespoon plain flour
½ pint milk
3 tablespoons cheese (grated)
salt and pepper
½ teaspoon made mustard
(French, or English)

Method

Cut fillet into portions. Well butter an ovenproof dish, put in the fish and a little salt and sprinkle well with lemon juice. Cover with buttered paper and poach in the oven at 350°F or Mark 4 for 12 minutes.

Boil spinach, drain, press and return to pan with ½ oz butter. Toss over the heat for 1-2 minutes, turn into an oven-proof serving dish. Arrange the fish on the top.

Prepare the mornay sauce, reserving a little cheese. Pour sauce over fish to coat it, sprinkle with the reserved cheese and brown in oven at 425°F or Mark 7, or under grill.

Scallops mornay

6 scallops
1 slice of onion
6 peppercorns
½ bayleaf
few parsley stalks
3-4 tablespoons water
creamed potatoes (for piping)

For mornay sauce
1 oz butter
1 oz plain flour
½ pint milk
liquid from scallops
2 rounded tablespoons grated
cheese—preferably half
Parmesan, half Gruyère

Method

After removing from shell, wash and dry scallops and place in a pan with onion, peppercorns, herbs and water. Cover and simmer for 5-6 minutes, then drain and reserve liquid.

To prepare sauce: melt butter in a pan, remove from heat, blend in flour and then milk. Stir over gentle heat until boiling, strain on the liquid from the scallops, boil to reduce for 2-3 minutes. Remove from the heat, allow to cool, then beat in the cheese a little at a time, re-serving 1 tablespoon.

Quarter the scallops and arrange in buttered shells or gratin dishes. Spoon over sauce, dust with cheese and brown in a hot oven, or under the grill.

You can pipe a thick border of creamed potatoes round the shells before setting them on a baking sheet for browning. Fix shells in place with a little creamed potato, or wedge them with a piece of raw potato.

Scalloped mushrooms

½-¾ lb flat mushrooms
2 tablespoons fresh white
  breadcrumbs
½ oz butter (melted)
1 egg yolk
1-2 tablespoons cream, or top of
  milk
1 rounded teaspoon finely
  chopped parsley
1 rounded teaspoon chives
1 clove of garlic (crushed with
  salt)
salt and pepper
mornay sauce (made with ½ oz
  butter, ½ oz flour, ½ pint
  milk, 1½ oz grated cheese,
  seasoning)
grated cheese (to sprinkle)
browned crumbs
extra melted butter

4-6 scallop shells

Method

Set oven at 350°F or Mark 4.
   Wash and peel mushrooms,
remove stalks, and set aside
3-4 for each person. Chop
stalks and peelings and any
remaining mushrooms. Add
fresh crumbs and bind with the
butter, egg yolk and cream; mix
in the herbs, garlic and seasoning. Fill the whole mushrooms
with this mixture and arrange
them in buttered scallop shells,
coat with mornay sauce.
Sprinkle with cheese, browned
crumbs and melted butter and
bake in pre-set moderate oven
for 12-15 minutes.

Mushrooms au gratin

1 lb mushrooms
1-1½ oz butter
salt and pepper
pinch of ground mace
cayenne pepper
2-3 tablespoons browned crumbs
2-3 tablespoons grated Parmesan
  cheese

For white sauce
1 oz butter
1 oz plain flour
7½ fl oz milk
2½ fl oz double cream

Method

Set oven at 400°F or Mark 6.
Trim, wash and dry the mushrooms, leaving on the stalks,
and fry briskly in the butter. Turn
into a gratin dish and season
with salt, pepper, mace and a
sprinkling of cayenne. Prepare
the white sauce, adding the
cream after sauce has boiled for
1 minute.
   Spoon sauce over mush-
rooms, dust with crumbs and
cheese (mixed) and bake in pre-
set oven for 7-10 minutes.

Omelet Germiny

6 eggs
1 large handful of sorrel
2 large handfuls of spinach
2½-3 oz butter
salt and pepper
1 small carton (2½ fl oz) double
  cream
½ pint mornay sauce
½ lb spring onions
Gruyère cheese (grated)

Method

Blanch the sorrel and spinach together, then drain, press and chop. Put this into a pan with 1 oz of the butter, season, cover and cook for 4-5 minutes. Take off the lid and increase the heat to drive off any moisture; add the cream and simmer un-covered for 2-3 minutes, then draw aside.

Note: if sorrel is not available (it can only be grown in a garden or gathered wild in the spring) use a good-size lettuce. Do not blanch this, but shred and cook straight away in butter with the spinach.

Prepare mornay sauce. Trim the onions, leaving on 1-2 inches of green, and blanch for 5-6 minutes, then drain and return to the pan with ½ oz of the butter. Simmer for 2-3 minutes. Break the eggs into a bowl, beat to a froth, season and add 2 tablespoons water. Make the omelet in the usual way, using the rest of the butter (see page 24, omitting cheese), and when creamily set spread the spinach mixture on top. Roll up and tip on to an oven-proof serving dish. Coat with the mornay sauce, sprinkle with the grated cheese and glaze under the grill. Garnish with the spring onions and serve the omelet at once.

Aubergine cream

4 medium-size aubergines
  (about 1½ lb)
6 oz cooked ham (half fat,
  half lean)
chopped parsley
4 eggs (separated)
scant 2 oz Gruyère cheese
  (grated)
salt and pepper
tomato sauce (for serving)

For béchamel sauce
1 oz butter
¾ oz plain flour
good ¼ pint flavoured milk
salt and pepper

Charlotte tin, or ring mould (1½ pints capacity)

Method

Peel aubergines, dice them and boil in pan of salted water for 4-5 minutes. When barely tender, drain aubergines thoroughly, then mash. Chop ham also and add to the aubergines with the parsley. Set oven at 400°F or Mark 6.

Make the béchamel sauce, stir in the egg yolks, and add the aubergine mixture, cheese and seasoning. Whip egg whites firmly and fold into the mixture. Turn it into the well greased tin (or mould) and cook in pre-set oven for about 25-30 minutes until well browned. Serve in the tin (or mould) or turn out, and pour round a tomato sauce.

Artichokes au gratin duxelles

2 lb jerusalem artichokes
milk and water (in equal pro-
   portions, enough to cover
   artichokes)
½ pint vegetable stock (from
   artichokes)
6 oz mushrooms (flat)
1 onion
1 oz butter
1 oz plain flour
salt and pepper
2-3 tablespoons creamy milk
1 tablespoon browned
   breadcrumbs
1-2 tablespoons grated cheese

Method

Peel artichokes and put them in a pan. Cover with milk and water mixture, simmer for 7-10 minutes, or until just tender, drain and put into an ovenproof gratin dish. Retain ½ pint of the artichoke liquid for the sauce.

Wash and chop mushrooms finely. Do not peel or remove the stalks. Chop the onion, melt butter in a pan, add onion and mushrooms, cover and cook slowly for 3-4 minutes. Then take off lid and boil hard to remove some of the moisture.

Draw aside, stir in the flour and pour on the artichoke liquid. Stir over heat until boiling and cook for 2 minutes. Season and finish with creamy milk. Spoon this sauce over the artichokes and scatter over some browned crumbs and then the grated cheese.

Cook for about 10 minutes, or until evenly browned, in an oven at 375-400°F or Mark 5-6.

If you prefer to use fewer artichokes, place a layer of sliced, hard-boiled egg at the bottom of the dish.

Gratin florentine

1 lb frozen leaf spinach
¼ pint milk
4 eggs (beaten)
4 egg yolks (beaten)
salt
pepper (ground from mill)
¼ pint single cream
little nutmeg (freshly grated)
8 oz long grain rice (cooked)
4 oz Cheddar cheese (grated)
1 oz Parmesan cheese (grated)

Method

Allow the spinach to thaw, press between 2 plates to remove the excess moisture, then chop finely. Set the oven at 375°F or Mark 5. Heat the milk, tip it on to the beaten eggs and yolks, season well and add the cream and nutmeg.

Butter an ovenproof dish and fill with layers of spinach, rice and Cheddar cheese, beginning and ending with spinach; pour over the egg mixture. Mix any remaining Cheddar cheese with the Parmesan and sprinkle this over the top. Cook au bain-marie in the pre-set oven till brown and crisp on the top, about 30 minutes.

Cauliflower au gratin

1 large cauliflower
1 bayleaf
3 tablespoons grated cheese
3 tablespoons fresh white bread-
    crumbs
½ oz butter

For mornay sauce
1½ oz butter
3 tablespoons plain flour
¾ pint milk
salt and pepper
3 tablespoons grated cheese
French, or English, mustard

When cooking cauliflower, add a bayleaf; this lessens the strong smell and gives a delicate flavour to the vegetable.

Method

Wash cauliflower thoroughly in salted water. Trim stalk but leave some green leaves on. Then break into sprigs (if necessary, use a knife to cut the stalk so that it remains attached to the sprigs and is not wasted) and boil for about 15 minutes, or until tender, in salted water with the bayleaf.

Meanwhile, prepare mornay sauce. Melt butter in a pan and stir in flour off the heat. Blend in milk, then stir until boiling. Cook for 2 minutes, season, draw on one side and cool before beating in the cheese by degrees. Then stir in the mustard to taste.

Watchpoint After mustard is added, do not boil the sauce because this will spoil the taste.

Now carefully drain cauliflower, butter a basin and arrange sprigs in it with the stalks towards the centre. When the basin is full, spoon in 2-3 tablespoons of sauce. Press down very lightly to bind the sprigs together and then invert the basin on to an ovenproof dish. Take off basin, spoon sauce over and around, mix cheese and crumbs together and scatter over the cauliflower. Sprinkle well with melted butter and brown in the oven for about 5 minutes at 400°F or Mark 6.

Cauliflower snow (Choufleur à la neige)

1 large cauliflower
1 large onion (sliced)
2 oz butter
2 tomatoes (scalded, skinned
    and sliced)
1 oz plain flour
½ pint milk
salt and pepper
6 oz Cheddar cheese (grated)
4 eggs (separated)

Method

Cut cauliflower into fleurettes and cook in boiling salted water, stems down, for 5-10 minutes. Sauté the onion in 1 oz butter until soft, add tomatoes and cook for 2-3 minutes.

Meanwhile make a sauce with the remaining butter, and the flour and milk; season and add 4 oz of the cheese. Arrange cauliflower in a gratin dish, spoon over the onion and tomato mixture and coat with sauce.

Beat the egg whites stiffly and arrange on top of cauliflower, making four pockets for the egg yolks. Drop a yolk into each pocket. Sprinkle over the remaining cheese and grill until crisp and golden-brown.

44

Endives ardennaise

5 good heads of chicory
2-3 tablespoons water
squeeze of lemon juice
little grated cheese and melted
   butter (for browning)

For sauce
good ½ oz butter
scant ½ oz plain flour
½ pint milk
1½ oz cheese (Gruyère and
   Parmesan mixed, or dry Cheddar)
   —grated
½ teaspoon French, or made
   English, mustard
salt and pepper
2 oz lean cooked ham (cut in
   julienne strips)

This recipe gets its name from the Belgian region of the Ardennes, famed for its ham. However, the ham in this recipe doesn't have to be ardennaise — any good lean ham may be used.

Method

Trim the chicory, put into a well-buttered flameproof casserole with the water and lemon juice. Cover with a piece of buttered paper and the lid. Set on a low heat for 5-6 minutes, then put into the oven pre-set at 350°F or Mark 4 for 45-50 minutes until the chicory is clear-looking and very tender.

Meanwhile prepare a sauce with the butter, flour and milk and beat in the cheese with the seasonings. Stir the ham into this sauce. Lift the chicory on to a serving dish, coat with the sauce, dust well with the grated cheese, sprinkle with melted butter and brown under the grill.

Cheese and potato fritters

1½ oz Parmesan cheese (grated)
¾ lb potatoes (cooked)
2 eggs (separated)
2 tablespoons double cream
salt and pepper
pinch of cayenne pepper
pinch of chopped parsley
pinch of curry powder (optional)

Method

Sieve the potatoes and keep hot. Beat the egg yolks, add to the cream and mix with the potatoes, cheese and seasoning. Beat the egg whites and fold into the mixture. Drop a tablespoon at a time into deep fat and fry until crisp.

Note: alternatively the egg whites may be omitted from the mixture, which could then be formed into cakes, coated lightly with flour, dipped in beaten egg and breadcrumbs, and fried in shallow fat.

Cheese and potato pancake

3 oz Cheddar cheese (grated)
8 good-sized potatoes (peeled
   and sliced into ¼-inch rounds)
little butter, or lard
salt and pepper

Method

Melt the butter or lard in a large frying pan and then arrange a third of the potato slices in the pan so that they overlap in circles. Sprinkle with salt, pepper and a third of the cheese. Add another layer of potato, cheese and potato and end with cheese. Cover with a lid or metal plate and cook over moderate heat for about 45 minutes, or until potatoes are soft. Loosen the potato cake from the pan with a palette knife and turn on to a serving dish.

Cheese and potato with tomato coulis

1½ lb potatoes (creamed)
2 oz cheese (grated)
grated rind of 1 orange
salt and pepper
chopped parsley (to finish)

For tomato coulis
1 lb tomatoes (skinned, seeds
   removed, flesh sliced)
1 Spanish onion (sliced in rings)
1 tablespoon oil, or dripping
good squeeze of orange juice
   (optional)

Method

To make the tomato coulis: fry the onion rings in oil or dripping until just brown. Add the prepared tomatoes and orange juice. Season, cover pan and cook for 2-3 minutes until tomatoes are just soft.

Mix the grated cheese and orange rind with the potato, arrange in a circle in a flameproof dish and brown lightly in a hot oven or under the grill. Put the tomato coulis in the centre.

Tomatoes au fromage

1 lb ripe tomatoes (skinned)
salt and pepper
3 shallots
3 oz cheese (grated Parmesan and
  Gruyère mixed)
2-3 tablespoons breadcrumbs
1½ oz butter

Method
Set the oven at 375°F or Mark 5.
Halve the tomatoes, flick out
seeds, season the halves and
arrange in an ovenproof dish.
Chop the shallots very finely and
scatter them over the tomatoes.
Add the cheese to the crumbs
and cover each tomato half with
this mixture. Melt the butter,
spoon it carefully over the
tomatoes and bake in the pre-set
moderately hot oven for about
10 minutes, until the tomatoes
are tender.

Lasagne (vegetarian)

2 cans (15 oz each) Italian
  tomatoes
1 can (2¼ oz) tomato purée
1 teaspoon dried marjoram
salt and pepper
1 teaspoon sugar
16 oz can Nuttolene (chopped)
4 oz lasagne
6 oz Ricotta, or cream, cheese
2 oz Parmesan cheese (grated)
8 oz Mozarella cheese (sliced)

Nuttolene is available from
health food shops and other
suppliers of vegetarian foods.

Method
Mix together the tomatoes,
tomato purée, marjoram, seasonings and sugar; simmer gently
for about 30 minutes. Add the
Nuttolene and continue to
simmer gently. Cook the lasagne
in boiling salted water for 10-15
minutes.
Mix all the cheeses together.
Set oven at 375°F or Mark 5.
Cover the base of an ovenproof dish with a layer of the
tomato mixture. Add half the
lasagne, then another layer of
sauce, then a layer of the
cheese mixture. Repeat these
layers with the remaining ingredients, finishing with a layer
of cheese. Bake near top of the
pre-set oven for 30 minutes
until golden-brown.

Pilaf (basic recipe)

6 oz long grain rice
2 oz butter
1 onion (thinly sliced, or chopped)
pinch of saffron (soaked in 2 tablespoons hot water for 30 minutes)
¾-1 pint stock
salt and pepper
1-2 oz dry cheese (grated)

Method

Heat a shallow saucepan or flameproof casserole. Add three-quarters of the butter, put in the onion, cook gently for 5 minutes, then add the rice and continue to cook gently for 2-3 minutes. Season well, pour on saffron liquid and about three-quarters of stock. Bring rice to boil, cover pan and put in oven at 350°F or Mark 4 for 15 minutes. Add a little more stock, if necessary, and cook for a further 5-7 minutes, when all stock should be absorbed and the rice tender.

Dot the surface of the rice with the rest of the butter and sprinkle with the cheese. Cover and leave on the top of the stove (not on heat), or in warming drawer, to keep warm. Stir rice lightly with a fork before turning into the serving dish.

Pilafs can be plain, with no additional flavouring other than a little onion, or have various ingredients added. A plain pilaf is best substituted for potatoes for accompanying any meat or chicken dishes, or it can be mixed with any leftovers of chicken, ham or fish.

Shredded ham, cooked chicken, raw chicken livers, etc. can also be added to the pilaf (when rice is added to onion).

A pilaf will keep hot satisfactorily for up to 30 minutes if covered and left on top of stove.

Risotto milanese

8 oz thick grain rice (preferably
    Italian)
1 marrow bone (optional)
2 oz butter
1 small onion (finely chopped)
1 clove of garlic (chopped, or
    crushed, with ½ teaspoon salt)
1 pinch of saffron (soaked in 2
    tablespoons hot water) — optional
salt and pepper
about 1¼ pints chicken, or veal,
    stock
2-3 tablespoons grated Parmesan
    cheese

Sliced mushrooms (2-3 oz) are
sometimes added to this risotto
with the onion. For special
occasions, use a glass of white
wine in place of the same
amount of stock.

The quantity of rice given here
is enough for a main course for
four people.

Method

Scoop out marrow from the
bone and cut in small pieces.
Melt a good half of the butter
in a shallow pan or flameproof
casserole, add marrow, onion
and garlic. Fry gently for 4-5
minutes, add rice and continue
to fry, stirring continually until
all the grains look white —
4-5 minutes.

Then add saffron in its liquid
and about a third of the stock.
Season and simmer, stirring
occasionally until the rice
thickens, then add another
third of the stock. Continue in
this way until the grains are
barely tender and the risotto
creamy.

Draw pan aside, dot the
surface with the remaining
butter and sprinkle with 1-2
tablespoons of Parmesan
cheese. Cover rice and leave
for 5 minutes, or until ready to
serve. Stir once or twice with a
fork, then turn into a hot dish.
Avoid touching with a spoon as
this makes it mushy.

Note: bone marrow is characteristic of a risotto milanese
but both it and the saffron may
be omitted. If more convenient,
the marrow bone may be boiled
before scooping out the marrow,
which is then added to the
risotto towards the end of
cooking. In either case the
bone can be used for stock.

Tagliatelle al prosciutto

8-12 oz tagliatelle
3 oz butter
about ½ lb green gammon bacon
  (diced)
3-4 sticks of celery (chopped)
1 carrot (chopped)
1-2 cloves of garlic (chopped)
1 rounded tablespoon tomato
  conserve (concentrated purée)
¼ pint jellied veal bone stock
salt and pepper
2 tablespoons grated Parmesan
  cheese

Method

Boil tagliatelle gently for 10-12 minutes, then drain and rinse. To keep it warm, pour hot water into the pan just to cover the bottom before putting back the tagliatelle; cover pan and leave in a warm place.

Melt two-thirds of the butter in a shallow pan, put in the bacon and fry gently for 3-4 minutes. Then add the vegetables and garlic, cover and cook for 4-5 minutes. Stir in the tomato conserve and stock. Season and continue to cook, uncovered, a further 5 minutes until syrupy.

Drain the tagliatelle and add the remaining butter, season and shake up over the heat until thoroughly hot, then add the cheese and turn on to a serving dish. Spoon the bacon mixture over the pasta.

Spaghetti alla carbonara

1 lb spaghetti
1 onion (finely sliced)
6 oz bacon (diced)
1½ oz butter
1 wineglass white wine
3 eggs
2 oz Parmesan cheese (grated)
1 rounded tablespoon chopped
  parsley
pepper (ground from mill)
½ oz butter

Method

Fry the onion and the bacon in the butter until golden-brown. Then tip on the wine and reduce until it has almost evaporated. Whisk the eggs and add the Parmesan, chopped parsley and pepper.

Cook the spaghetti in plenty of boiling salted water for 12-15 minutes and then drain thoroughly, add the ½ oz butter. Mix the spaghetti with the egg mixture in a clean bowl, add the onion and bacon mixture, reheat until thickening creamily, then serve at once.

Ravioli with spinach and curd cheese filling

10 oz plain flour
½ teaspoon salt
1½ tablespoons olive oil
2 eggs (beaten)
3-4 tablespoons milk, or water

For filling
1 small packet of frozen spinach
    purée, or ½-¾ lb fresh spinach
2 oz curd, or cream, cheese
salt and pepper
small pinch of ground mace, or
    grated nutmeg

Method

Sift the flour with salt on to a laminated plastic work top or board, make a well in the centre and put in the oil, eggs and half the milk or water.

Start mixing in the oil, eggs and water gradually, drawing in the flour; add the rest of the liquid as it is needed. Continue to work up the paste until it is smooth and firm, knead well, then cover with a cloth and leave for 20-30 minutes to get rid of any elasticity. Cut in half and roll out one piece, paper thin. Slide to one side, then roll out the second piece as thinly.

To make filling: if using frozen spinach, put into a pan and cook gently, stirring occasionally until firm. If fresh, boil, drain and dry; sieve to a purée or chop very finely. Sieve cheese and mix in the spinach when cold. Season well and add spice. The mixture should be a firm purée.

Brush paste with water and put out the filling in teaspoons at regular intervals on the paste. Lift the first piece on top and with a small ball of the paste press down the top piece around each mound of filling. Stamp out each one with a small fluted cutter or cut out in squares with a pastry wheel. Leave for 2-3 hours to dry a little. To cook, simmer in stock or water for 15-20 minutes; drain and cover ravioli with a good tomato sauce. Continue to simmer until golden. Serve well drained with grated cheese.

Tomato sauce

1 lb tomatoes, or 1 medium-size
    can tomatoes
1 small onion (sliced)
1 oz butter, or 2 tablespoons oil
1 clove of garlic (chopped)
good pinch of dried mixed herbs
1 wineglass stock, or water
salt and pepper
tomato purée
½ oz butter

Method

Wipe tomatoes, cut in half and squeeze out seeds. Slice and put into a pan with the onion, butter and garlic. Add herbs and stock or water, season well, cover and cook to a pulp. Rub through a strainer, return to the rinsed out pan and add a little tomato purée to strengthen the flavour. Use your own judgment as to the amount, as this depends on the ripeness of the tomatoes. Add butter and boil until thick, stirring frequently.

When tomatoes are plentiful a double quantity can be made (or more) as it will keep for about a week in a covered container in the refrigerator, or can be deep frozen.

French gnocchi (Gnocchi parisienne)

6 fl oz milk
3 oz butter
4½ oz plain flour (sifted)
3 eggs
2-2½ oz cheese (grated)
salt and pepper
pinch of mustard
good ½ pint mornay sauce

This is made like choux pastry but is poached before coating with a mornay sauce. It is then baked (and puffs up in the same way as choux pastry). Well made, it is light and delicious and very suitable for a lunch dish with green salad, or for a savoury.

Method

Bring milk and butter to the boil, draw pan aside and pour in the flour all at once (this is easier if the flour has been sifted on to a piece of paper first). Beat until the mixture is smooth; cool, then beat in the eggs, one at a time. (This can conveniently be done in an electric mixer, on the paddle, at slow speed.) When the paste appears well beaten and slightly glossy, stir in cheese, season to taste and add mustard.

Watchpoint At this stage the paste can be left, covered, for some hours, or overnight if more convenient. Once poached, it can also be left in the dish for some time before being coated with the sauce and baked.

To poach, take 2 dessert-spoons and have ready a large pan of salted water at simmering

French gnocchi after being baked in the oven with mornay sauce

point. Dip the spoons in this until hot, then fill one spoon well with the mixture and with the other spoon smooth over the top to form mixture into an oval. Make sure there are no cracks: to avoid this, dig down in the mixture to get a really full spoonful. Once shaped, hold the spoon containing the mixture in the simmering water, tapping the tip gently on the bottom of the pan 2-3 times. The gnocchi will then detach itself. Continue in this way until all the mixture has been used or until the pan is fairly full. The gnocchi do not swell during poaching, but allow them room to be turned or turn themselves. Taking the time from when the last one was put in, allow 12 minutes for poaching. During the cooking, the water must just tremble, no more. Shake the pan gently from time to time.

When cooked, they are quite firm to the touch and look a little spongy. Lift them out carefully on to absorbent paper or muslin. When all are poached, arrange them in a well-buttered ovenproof dish. The easiest way to transfer the gnocchi is to tilt the paper so that each one falls gently into the spoon.

When they are ready to be baked, spoon over the mornay sauce and sprinkle with a little additional cheese. Bake in a rather hot oven, pre-set at 375-400°F or Mark 5-6, for about 40 minutes, or until well-risen and brown. Take them out of the oven and leave for a few minutes before serving; the gnocchi will subside a little, which makes for a better texture.

Gnocchi romana

1 medium-size onion
1 bayleaf
½ pint milk
½ pint water
5 rounded tablespoons maize
    meal, or coarse semolina
salt and pepper
½ teaspoon French mustard
1 oz butter
2 oz cheese (grated)
½ pint tomato sauce (see page 51),
    or mornay sauce

Method

Put onion, bayleaf, milk and water into a pan, cover and bring very slowly to the boil. Strain and set aside.

Draw pan aside and stir in the maize meal (or semolina). Return pan to heat and stir until boiling; season and if too thick add more liquid. The consistency should be that of thick porridge.

Continue to simmer, stirring frequently, for 7-10 minutes. Draw pan aside, adjust seasoning, then add mustard, butter and three-quarters of the grated cheese. Turn out on to a tray or flat dish so that the mixture spreads to a thickness of ½-¾ inch. Leave for 2-3 hours.

Turn the sheet of gnocchi on to a board or table and cut it into small squares, rounds or crescents. Arrange these in a well-buttered ovenproof dish in a circle, with the pieces over-lapping, leaving a well in the centre. Sprinkle gnocchi generously with melted butter and scatter on the remaining cheese. Brown in a quick oven, pre-set at 400°F or Mark 6, for 10-15 minutes. Pour sauce into the dish to cover the bottom well. Serve rest of sauce separately.

Tortelli

8 oz Ricotta, or curd, cheese
2 oz Parmesan cheese (grated)
1 egg
1 egg yolk
salt and pepper
pinch of allspice
1 tablespoon chopped parsley
ravioli paste (quantity made
    with 12 oz flour) — see page 51
2-3 tablespoons melted butter
1-2 tablespoons grated
    Parmesan cheese

Method

Mix the cheeses together and beat until smooth, then add the egg and egg yolk, seasonings and parsley. Roll out the paste very thinly, stamp into rounds about 2½ inches in diameter. Put 1 teaspoon of cheese mixture in the centre of each round, brush round the edge with water and fold over like a turnover, press edges down firmly and leave for 30 minutes.

Have ready a large pan of boiling salted water, put in the little turnovers and simmer for 15-20 minutes. Then lift out with a draining spoon, drain well on a cloth or piece of muslin, turn on to a dish, spoon the melted butter over them and dust well with the Parmesan cheese. Serve very hot.

Cheese, bacon and potato galette

4 oz sliced processed cheese
4 oz streaky bacon (No. 4 cut)
2 lb potatoes
1 oz butter
salt and pepper
½-¾ pint chicken stock

Method

Remove the rind from bacon, spread out rashers with a heavy knife and cut each in half. Cut each slice of cheese in four. Peel the potatoes and cut in thin slices about the thickness of a shilling.

Rub half the butter around an ovenproof dish and arrange potatoes in it, seasoning lightly between layers. Pour over stock to come almost to the top of potatoes, cover with bacon and cheese and dot over the remaining butter. Bake in a hot oven, 400°F or Mark 6, for about 1¼ hours, or until potatoes are quite tender and the cheese and bacon brown and crisp.

Cheese and bacon waffles

2 oz Cheddar cheese (grated)
streaky bacon rashers
8 oz plain flour
1 teaspoon bicarbonate of soda
2 teaspoons baking powder
large pinch of salt
2 eggs
3 oz butter (melted)
¾ pint soured milk, or buttermilk

This recipe makes about 8 waffles.

Method

First heat the waffle iron.

Sift the flour with the bicarbonate of soda, baking powder and salt into a mixing bowl, make a well in the centre and put the eggs and melted butter in this. Start adding the soured milk to the eggs and whisk gently, or mix with a wooden spoon. Draw in the flour very gradually and continue beating until mixture is quite smooth and all the milk has been added. Fold in the cheese.

Pour the mixture from a small jug or spoon into the centre of the hot waffle iron, lay thin strips of streaky bacon over the batter, cover and leave closed until the steaming stops. The waffles should be puffed and golden-brown. Serve hot with pats of butter.

Ham au gratin

cooked ham
2 tablespoons white wine
½ pint white sauce
1 teaspoon French mustard
2 tablespoons grated Parmesan
    cheese
1 tablespoon browned crumbs

Method

Slice the cold ham fairly thinly and place in the bottom of a buttered ovenproof dish. Overlap the slices quite well as this will allow the sauce to flow between and under, as well as over, the ham. Then moisten the slices with the white wine.

Prepare the white sauce. Season it with the French mustard and only 1 tablespoon of the cheese. Stir sauce over gentle heat until well blended, but do not allow it to reboil.

Spoon sauce over the ham, mix the remaining cheese with the crumbs and scatter this over the top. Put the dish, uncovered, in moderate oven, preset at 350°F or Mark 4, for 30 minutes.

Spaghetti and ham au gratin

8 oz spaghetti
4 oz ham, or pork luncheon meat
(cut in dice, or julienne strips)
2 tablespoons tomato chutney
¾ oz butter
½ oz plain flour
2 teaspoons English mustard
(mixed to a paste with cold
water)
¼ pint water
¼ pint milk
salt and pepper
2 eggs (beaten)
1 oz Cheddar cheese (grated)

Pie dish (1½-2 pints capacity)

This dish can be prepared in advance and baked just before serving.

Method

Cook the spaghetti in plenty of boiling salted water until tender (12-15 minutes). Drain, refresh with a jug of hot water and drain again. Return the spaghetti to the saucepan and cover with warm water while preparing the other ingredients.

Butter the pie dish and set oven at 375°F or Mark 5. Mix the ham (or pork luncheon meat) with the tomato chutney and keep on one side.

Melt the butter in a pan, blend in the flour and cook very gently until straw-coloured and marbled in appearance. Blend in the made mustard, water and milk. Season and stir until boiling. Tip mixture into a bowl and allow to cool. Then add the beaten eggs. Drain the spaghetti again and mix in the mustard sauce; turn into buttered pie dish, layering it with the ham mixture. Cover the top with the grated cheese and bake in the pre-set oven until set and brown on the top (about 30 minutes).

Stuffed cabbage pancakes

½ pint pancake batter
½ pint mornay sauce

For filling
1 small, or ½ large, Dutch cabbage (the hard white variety, sometimes called salad cabbage, weighing about 1½ lb)
1 onion (sliced)
1 oz butter
4 oz salt belly pork (cooked until tender and cut in strips), or un smoked streaky bacon (cut in lardons and blanched)
4 tablespoons stock
salt and pepper

Method

Prepare the batter and leave to stand in a cool place for 30 minutes. Cook pancakes as for basic recipe and set aside.

Trim the cabbage, cut in four, discarding hard centre stalk, and shred finely. Put onion in a heavy flameproof casserole or pan with the butter, cover and cook slowly until soft. Add the pork or bacon to the pan and cook until golden-brown. Stir in the cabbage and stock, season to taste, cover with a buttered paper and a lid and cook slowly on top of the stove or in the oven at 350°F or Mark 4 until tender (for about 40 minutes).

Prepare the mornay sauce reserving 1 tablespoon cheese. Fill the pancakes with the cabbage mixture, fold them in half and place in a buttered ovenproof dish. Coat with mornay sauce, sprinkle with the reserved cheese and bake in pre-set oven at 400°F or Mark 6 for 7-10 minutes or until golden-brown.

Basic pancake batter

4 oz plain flour
pinch of salt
1 egg
1 egg yolk
½ pint milk
1 tablespoon melted butter, or salad oil

This recipe makes ½ pint batter.

Method

Sift the flour with the salt into a bowl, make a well in the centre, add the egg and yolk and begin to add the milk slowly, stirring all the time. When half the milk has been added, stir in the melted butter or oil and beat well until smooth.

Add the remaining milk and leave to stand for 30 minutes before using. The batter should have the consistency of thin cream — if too thick, add a little extra milk.

To cook the pancakes, use a small pan about 6 inches in diameter. Wipe out the pan and set over moderate heat. When thoroughly hot put in a few drops of oil. Take 1 tablespoon of the batter and tip this into the pan, immediately rolling it round clock-wise to coat the bottom evenly. Cook until the underside of the pancake is a good brown colour, flip it over with a palette knife and cook for about 10 seconds on the other side. Stack the pancakes one on top of the other until you are ready to use them.

Roquefort salad

1¼ lb small new potatoes
4-6 oz thin streaky bacon rashers
   (green)

For dressing
2 oz Roquefort cheese
7 tablespoons French dressing
salt and pepper
¼ pint double cream
watercress (to garnish)

Method
Boil the potatoes in their skins.
Meanwhile, shred the bacon
and fry until crisp. Peel the
potatoes while still hot, slice
and moisten with some of the
French dressing. Add the crispy
pieces of bacon and season.

Crush the Roquefort well and
work in remainder of French
dressing and the cream. Dish up
potatoes and coat with dressing.
Garnish with watercress.

Roquefort and walnut salad

2 lettuces (hearts only)
3 slices of white bread
1½ oz Roquefort, or other
   blue cheese (crushed)
6 large walnuts, or 12 half-
   kernels
8 tablespoons French dressing

Method
Wash and dry lettuces, chill
until crisp. Cut crusts from
bread and toast until golden-
brown. When cold cut each
slice into four and spread with
the crushed Roquefort. Shell
walnuts and, if wished, blanch
kernels to remove skins.

Just before serving mix
lettuce, walnuts and Roquefort
'toasts' with the French dressing.

French dressing

Mix 1 tablespoon wine, or
tarragon, vinegar with ½
teaspoon each of salt and
freshly ground black pep-
per and freshly chopped
herbs if wished. Add 3
tablespoons of salad oil.

When dressing thickens,
taste for correct seasoning;
if it is sharp yet oily, add
more salt. Quantities should
be in the ratio of 1 part
vinegar to 3 parts oil.

Pear and Roquefort salad

4 ripe dessert pears
2 oz Roquefort cheese
½-1 oz butter
little single cream, or top
 of milk
3-4 tablespoons cream cheese
salt and pepper
4 lettuce leaves
paprika pepper (to serve)

Method

Peel and core the pears. Cream
the Roquefort cheese with the
butter to the consistency of
whipped cream and fill the middle of the pears. Whisk a little
cream or milk into the cream
cheese until the mixture will just
pour; season lightly. Place each
pear on a lettuce leaf, coat with
the cream cheese dressing and
dust with paprika. Serve chilled
with bread and butter.

Tomatoes with Roquefort cream

8 even-size tomatoes
salt and pepper
2 eggs (hard-boiled)
3 sticks of tender celery (taken
 from centre of the head) —
 finely diced
3 oz Roquefort cheese
2 tablespoons double cream
4 tablespoons French dressing
1 teaspoon chopped chives

Method

Scald and skin tomatoes. Cut
off the tops from the smooth
end and carefully scoop out the
seeds and core, using a teaspoon, drain and season the
insides.

Chop the whites of the hard-
boiled eggs and mix with the
celery. Sieve the cheese and
work half with the cream in a
bowl. Combine celery mixture
with this cheese and fill into the
tomatoes; replace the tops of
the tomatoes 'on the slant'.
Work the French dressing into
the remaining cheese and add
the chives.

Sieve the egg yolks on to a
serving dish, set tomatoes on
top and spoon over the dressing.

Mushroom and Gruyère salad

½ lb white button mushrooms
olive oil (to sauté)
French dressing (to moisten) —
    see page 58
1 shallot (finely chopped)
6 oz broad beans (weighed when
    shelled)
6 oz Gruyère cheese
lettuce, or watercress

Method

Wash and wipe mushrooms, sauté quickly in a little olive oil. Set aside, and moisten with French dressing while still hot. Add the shallot. Leave to get cold. Cook beans and remove the outer jackets, set aside. Cut the Gruyère into match-size pieces and add to the mushrooms with the broad beans. Add more dressing if necessary, and season well. Arrange the salad on a dish surrounded with well-washed lettuce or watercress.

Avocado pears with Roquefort dressing

2-3 avocado pears (according to
    size)
1 small lettuce

For dressing
2 oz Roquefort cheese
1 teaspoon Worcestershire
    sauce
2 tablespoons double cream
4-5 tablespoons French dressing
    (see page 58)
½ teaspoon finely grated onion

Method

First prepare the dressing. Work the Roquefort until quite smooth, adding the Worcestershire sauce and cream, then gradually the French dressing and finely grated onion.

Prepare the lettuce and arrange in a dish or on individual plates. Peel and quarter the avocado pears, arrange on the lettuce leaves, spoon over the dressing and serve.

Tomatoes Gervais

8 tomatoes
salt and pepper
4 oz cream cheese (2 packets
    Gervais, or loose curd cheese, or
    home-made)
small bunch fresh chives (or
    chopped parsley, or spring
    onion tops, or snipped watercress
    stalks)
2-3 tablespoons double cream,
    or top of milk
watercress (to garnish) – optional
French dressing (see page 58)

A curd cheese such as Gervais is
best to use here as it is richer
than cottage cheese, but not as
rich as the Petit-Suisse type of
full cream cheese.

If neither fresh chives nor the
A.F.D. (accelerated freeze dried)
ones are available and the alter-
natives are used, then chopped
herbs, such as thyme, marjoram
or basil, should be added to the
dressing.

Method

Scald and skin the tomatoes by
placing them in a bowl, pouring
boiling water over them, count-
ing 12 before pouring off the
hot water and replacing it with
cold. The skin then comes off
easily. Cut a slice from the top
(not stalk end) of each tomato,
reserve slices; hold tomato in
hollow of your palm, flick out
seeds with the handle of a teaspoon, using the bowl of the
spoon to detach the core. So
much the better if the spoon is
worn and therefore slightly
sharp. Drain the hollowed-out
tomatoes and lightly season inside each one with salt.

Sieve the cheese by pushing it
through a strainer resting on a
bowl, using a wooden spoon
or plastic spatula. Season well
and add some of the chives (cut
finely with scissors), or chopped
herbs. Soften with cream or top
of milk.

Fill the tomatoes with this
cheese mixture using a teaspoon, replace their top slices
on the slant and arrange them in
a serving dish.

Spoon a little French dressing
over the tomatoes (be sure to
reserve some for spooning over
at the last moment). Chill up
to 2 hours before serving. Garnish with watercress and
sprinkle remaining chives over
tomatoes.

Pancakes Beatrix

For batter
3½ oz plain flour
pinch of salt
2 eggs
2 tablespoons melted butter, or
    salad oil
¼-½ pint milk
1 oz Gouda cheese (finely grated)

For filling
2-3 smoked trout
béchamel sauce (made with 1 oz
    butter, 1 oz flour, ½ pint
    flavoured milk)
salt and pepper
1 teaspoon horseradish cream
1 tablespoon double cream

For finishing
3 tablespoons double cream
1 tablespoon grated Parmesan
    cheese

Method

Make the batter as in basic recipe (page 57), adding the grated cheese when half the milk has been added. Leave to stand for 30 minutes in a cool place.

Remove the skin and bone from the trout and divide into neat fillets. Make béchamel sauce, season, then add the horseradish cream and table-spoon of double cream.

Set the oven at 375°F or Mark 5. Fry paper-thin pan-cakes, fill each one with the fillets and sauce, roll up like cigars and arrange in a buttered dish. Spoon over the extra cream, dust with Parmesan cheese and bake in the pre-set oven for about 10 minutes. Serve very hot.

Gruyère pancakes

For batter
3½ oz plain flour
2 eggs
pinch of salt
8-10 fl oz milk and water (mixed)
1 dessertspoon olive oil
1 dessertspoon butter (melted)
1¾ oz Gruyère, or Cheddar,
    cheese (grated)

For filling
¾ pint thick béchamel sauce
    (made with 1¾ oz butter, 1½ oz
    flour, ¾ pint flavoured milk)
salt and pepper

To finish
1½ oz cheese (half Parmesan
    and half Gruyère, or sharp
    Cheddar) — grated
¾ oz butter
1 tablespoon chopped parsley

These pancakes can also be made with chopped ham, or mushrooms or cheese stirred into the filling.

Method

Prepare the batter, adding the oil, butter and Gruyère cheese when half the liquid has been added. Leave batter to stand for 30 minutes in a cool place before cooking the pancakes.

To prepare filling: make the béchamel sauce and season well. Keep warm.

Set oven at 400°F or Mark 6. Fry the pancakes.

Spread a good tablespoon of sauce on each pancake and roll them up like cigars. Place them in a buttered ovenproof dish and sprinkle with grated cheese. Dot pancakes with butter and brown in oven for about 7-10 minutes. Sprinkle with chopped parsley and serve very hot.

Entertaining with cheese

Don't forget cheese when you have a special meal to prepare; a little makes all the difference. For many of the dishes in this section cheese is the finishing touch rather than the main ingredient. But what a finishing touch! Cheese adds the distinctive flavour that turns an ordinary meat dish into a rich delight.

A delicious taste of luxury is introduced when cheese is added to a pastry dough, or when a mornay sauce coats a joint of tender veal. Vegetables and fish love the treatment too—cheese is such a versatile food it adapts to any flavour and enhances it.

The biggest luxury is of course the Swiss dish, a cheese fondue. Make this the centrepiece at your next party and the occasion will be a memorable one for all your friends. The Swiss know how to eat well and this dish is a delicious mixture of the best cheese and wines, a real gourmet's treat.

Cucumber and cheese mousse

1 large cucumber
6 oz curd, or cream, cheese
1 teaspoon onion juice (from
   finely grated onion)
salt and white pepper
¼ pint boiling water, or vegetable,
   or chicken, stock
½ oz gelatine (soaked in 3
   tablespoons cold water)
2 tablespoons white wine
   vinegar
1 tablespoon caster sugar
pinch of ground mace, or
   coriander
¼ pint double cream (lightly
   whipped)

For garnish
1 bunch of watercress
1 large green pepper
¼ pint French dressing
   (see page 58)

Ring mould (1½-2 pints capacity)

Method

Oil the ring mould. Dice cucumber finely, sprinkle with salt and dégorger. Work the cheese with onion juice and seasoning. Pour boiling water (or stock) on to soaked gelatine, stir until dissolved, then add cheese.

Drain the diced cucumber thoroughly and mix it with vinegar, sugar and spice. When the cheese mixture is quite cold, fold in the cucumber and the cream. Pour into the prepared mould and leave to set.

Wash and pick over the watercress. Chop the green pepper, blanch in boiling water and refresh it.

Turn out the mousse. Fill the centre with watercress. Add the green pepper to the French dressing and serve this separately with brown bread and butter.

Cod's roe pâté

12 oz smoked cod's roe (in the piece), or an 8 oz jar
1 teaspoon onion juice (from grated onion)
¼ pint olive oil
1 cup fresh white breadcrumbs, or 3-4 slices of bread
1 Demi-Sel cheese
lemon, or tomato, juice (to taste)
pepper

To garnish
toast (hot, dry)
unsalted butter
black olives
lemon quarters

Method

Scrape the roe from the skin and put in a bowl with the onion juice. Pour the oil over the breadcrumbs and leave to soak for 5 minutes (if using slices of bread, remove the crust, put bread in a dish and sprinkle with the oil). Pound or beat the cod's roe with the Demi-Sel cheese until quite smooth, then work in the breadcrumbs and oil, a little at a time. Finish with lemon (or tomato) juice to taste and season with pepper. The mixture should be light and creamy.

Pile into a shallow dish and serve with hot dry toast (served between the folds of a napkin), unsalted butter, black olives and quarters of lemon in separate dishes.

1 *Scraping piece of smoked cod's roe from skin into a mortar*
2 *Pounding together the roe and Demi-Sel cheese, while breadcrumbs soak*
3 *Dishing up the pâté ready to serve with toast, olives and lemon*

The finished cod's roe pâté is a light, creamy mixture

Courgettes maison

8 small courgettes
4 tomatoes
1 oz butter
1 shallot (finely chopped)
1 teaspoon paprika pepper
salt and pepper
½ lb shelled prawns
1 tablespoon grated Parmesan
 cheese (for dusting)

For mornay sauce
1 oz butter
1 oz plain flour
½ pint milk
2 oz Parmesan cheese (grated)

1 *Carefully scooping out the flesh of the cooked courgettes with a teaspoon*
2 *Filling courgette cases with the prawn and tomato mixture before spooning over mornay sauce and browning in oven*

Method

Trim each end of the courgettes, cook whole for 5 minutes in boiling salted water, then drain and refresh them. Remove a thin slice lengthways from each courgette, carefully scoop out the flesh with the point of a teaspoon and chop it. Scald and skin the tomatoes; cut in four, discard the seeds and chop flesh coarsely.

Melt the butter in a saucepan, add the chopped shallot and cook, covered, until quite soft but not brown; add the paprika, chopped courgette flesh and tomatoes. Season and cook briskly for 2-3 minutes. Stir in the prawns.

Put the courgette cases in a buttered gratin dish and fill them with the tomato and prawn mixture. Prepare mornay sauce in the usual way and spoon it over the courgettes; dust with cheese. Brown in quick oven at 425°F or Mark 7 for 10-12 minutes.

Courgettes maison is a delicious starter to a party meal

Eggs Connaught

6 hard-boiled eggs
¼ pint milk
1 slice of onion
blade of mace
6 peppercorns
3½ oz butter
1 tablespoon plain flour
salt and pepper
1 packet Demi-Sel cheese
1 teaspoon paprika
4 oz prawns (shelled)
½ bunch of watercress (to garnish)

Method

Scald the milk with the onion, mace and peppercorns, tip into a jug, cover and leave to infuse. Rinse the pan with cold water, drop in ½ oz butter, heat gently and blend in the flour. Strain on the milk and add salt. Stir continuously, bring milk to the boil, cook 1 minute. Turn on to a plate, cover with buttered paper to prevent a skin forming and leave sauce until cold. Cream remaining butter until soft.

Split the hard-boiled eggs in two, scoop out the yolks and rub through a wire strainer; keep the whites in a bowl of water as they soon get hard if exposed to air. Work the yolks with the butter, cheese, paprika and cold sauce. Chop half the prawns finely, add to the mixture and season to taste. Drain and dry the egg whites and have ready a round serving dish or use a cake platter.

Spoon a drop of filling on to the dish to hold each egg white in position, arrange them in a circle and then fill each with the mixture, or you can use a piping bag with a ½-inch plain pipe. Scatter over the remaining prawns (split in half, if large) and dust with paprika. Place the watercress in the middle and serve brown bread and butter separately.

For a very special party this recipe can be prepared with smoked salmon in place of prawns. Save a little smoked salmon to cut into fine shreds and scatter over.

While rubbing yolks through a strainer, keep whites in cold water

Prawn gougère

For choux pastry
¼ pint water
2 oz butter
2½ oz plain flour (sifted)
2 eggs (beaten)
2 oz Cheddar cheese (diced)
salt and pepper

For filling
8 oz prawns (shelled)
1 medium-size onion (sliced)
½ oz butter
1 dessertspoon plain flour
½ pint stock, or milk
1 teaspoon chopped parsley
2 tomatoes (skinned, seeds
    removed, and shredded)
chopped parsley (to garnish)
1 tablespoon finely grated
    Parmesan cheese
1 tablespoon browned crumbs

*Deep 8-inch diameter pie plate, or
ovenproof dish, or 6 small individual cocottes*

Gougère is a savoury choux
pastry dish mixed with cheese
and served plain, or with a
savoury filling.

Method

Prepare the choux pastry by
bringing ¼ pint water and the
butter to the boil, draw pan
aside, add the sifted flour all
at once, then stir vigorously
until paste is smooth. Cool,
then add the eggs, a little
at a time, beating them in
thoroughly. Stir in the cheese
and season.

To prepare filling: slice the
onion and cook it slowly in the
butter until soft. Draw the pan
aside, stir in the flour and pour
in the stock (or milk), stir until
boiling.

Take pan off the heat and
add the prawns, parsley and
shredded tomatoes. Set oven
at 400°F or Mark 6. Well
butter the pie plate (or ovenproof dish or cocottes), arrange
the choux pastry around the
sides, hollowing out the centre.
Pour the filling into this, dust
with grated cheese and crumbs
mixed together. Bake in pre-set
moderately hot oven for 30-40
minutes (or 15-20 minutes for
individual cocottes). When
choux is well risen and evenly
browned, take gougère out of
oven and sprinkle well with the
chopped parsley before serving.

Omelet Barante

6-8 eggs
1 small freshly cooked lobster
  (poached in court bouillon – see
  page 36)
6 oz firm white mushrooms
2-3 oz butter
salt and pepper
2½ fl oz port
1 small carton (2½ fl oz) double
  cream
½ pint light mornay sauce (made
  with milk flavoured as for
  béchamel sauce)
3-4 tablespoons freshly grated
  Parmesan cheese

The Baron de Barante was a famous 19th century gourmet and historian.

Method

Crack claws and remove shell from lobster. Cut the tail meat into scallops. Wipe the mushrooms, trim stalks level with the caps and slice evenly. Sauté these in half the butter for 4-5 minutes, then season lightly. Add port, cover and reduce to half quantity, draw aside and pour in the cream. Add the lobster meat, cover and simmer for 4-5 minutes, then draw aside.

Prepare the mornay sauce. Break the eggs into a bowl and beat to a light froth, add 2 tablespoons water and season. Make the omelet in the usual way, using the rest of the butter. While it is still soft and creamy in the middle spoon in the lobster mixture, then roll up and turn on to an ovenproof dish for serving. Coat at once with the sauce, sprinkle well with the freshly grated cheese and brown under the grill. Use the head shell and tail meat of lobster to garnish the dish – or use small lobsters, if available.

Spooning lobster and mushroom filling into the omelet Barante before rolling it up

Turning the finished omelet Barante on to a serving dish

Omelet Barante is shown here with a garnish of small lobsters

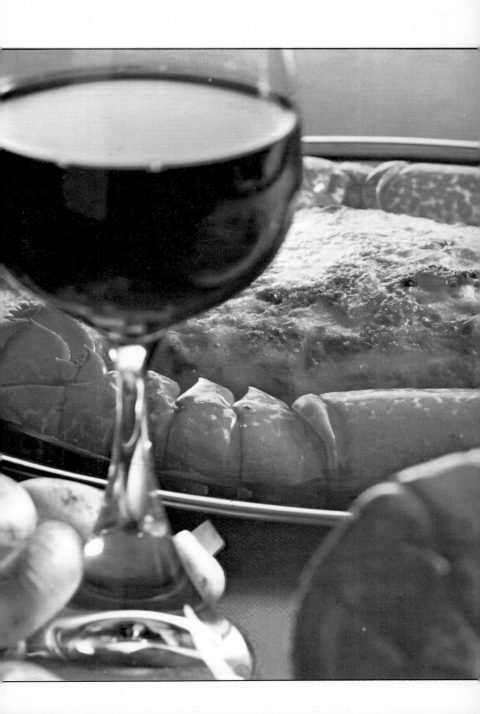

Cod Cubat

1½-2 lb cod fillet
salt and pepper
juice of ½ small lemon
8 oz flat mushrooms
½ oz butter
1 dessertspoon chopped mixed
 herbs
pinch of ground mace

For thick béchamel sauce
1 oz butter
2 tablespoons plain flour
¼ pint flavoured milk (infused
 with 3 peppercorns, ½ bayleaf,
 1 blade of mace)
salt and pepper

For mornay sauce
¾ oz butter
1 rounded tablespoon plain flour
½ pint milk
1½ oz cheese (Cheddar, or half
 Parmesan, half Gruyère) – grated
salt and pepper

To finish
1 teaspoon grated Parmesan
 cheese
1 French roll (for croûtes)
oil, or butter (for frying)

Method

Fillet the fish, remove the skin, then cut each piece in three. Buying and preparing the fish in this way gives the best-shaped portion of fish to serve between two sauces.

Place the fish in a well-buttered ovenproof dish, season and sprinkle with lemon juice; cover with buttered paper and cook in oven at 275°F or Mark 1 for 15 minutes.

Prepare béchamel sauce.

Wash and finely chop the mushrooms, without removing peel or stalks, and sauté in butter in a pan until dry; add seasoning, herbs and mace, mix with the béchamel sauce and set pan aside. Prepare the mornay sauce.

Reheat the mushroom mixture and spread down the centre of the serving dish, arrange the fish on top and coat with the mornay sauce. Sprinkle with Parmesan cheese and glaze under the grill just before serving.

Slice the roll and fry until golden-brown. Garnish dish with these croûtes.

Watchpoint If this dish is to be baked ahead of time and re-heated, mix a dessertspoon of browned crumbs with the cheese sprinkled on top to prevent pools of grease forming.

Placing the cooked pieces of cod on the mushroom mixture in the serving dish, before pouring over mornay sauce and glazing.

Délices of sole Parmesan

1½-2 lb lemon, or Dover, sole
   (filleted)
1 tablespoon seasoned flour
1 egg (beaten)
4 tablespoons fresh breadcrumbs
2 tablespoons grated Parmesan
   cheese
3 oz butter (clarified)
2 small bananas

½ oz butter
juice of ¼ lemon
8 almonds (blanched and shredded)

►

Délices of sole Parmesan continued

Method

Cut the fillets of fish into thick finger-like strips and dry them well. Roll them in the seasoned flour, brush with egg and coat with the breadcrumbs and cheese mixed together, pressing them on to the fish with a palette knife. Then fry fillets in the clarified butter until crisp and golden-brown. Pile them into a hot serving dish (without draining) and keep warm.

Wipe out the frying pan with absorbent paper. Cut the bananas in thick slanting slices, drop the ½ oz butter in the pan and, when foaming, add the bananas and fry quickly until brown. Pour over the lemon juice and add the almonds. Arrange the bananas and almonds around the fish and serve very hot.

Cutting the sole fillets into thick strips. The breadcrumbs and cheese mixture is used for coating the fish strips

Escalopes de veau au fromage

4 veal escalopes, or chops
1 oz butter
salt and pepper
2½ fl oz white wine, or veal
    stock, or chicken stock
4 slices (approximately 3 oz)
    Bel Paese, or Gruyère, cheese

For cream sauce
1 oz butter
scant oz plain flour
7½ fl oz milk
1 teaspoon French mustard
2 tablespoons single cream

Method

Sauté the escalopes or chops in the butter until golden-brown on both sides, allowing 8-10 minutes for escalopes and 10-12 minutes for chops. Season and pour on the wine (or stock), continue to cook until most of the liquid has evaporated. Lay the slices of cheese on the top of the meat.

Prepare the sauce as for white sauce and season with salt, pepper and French mustard. Add the cream. Coat this sauce over the veal and glaze under a hot grill before serving.

Escalopes of veal italienne

4-5 escalopes
1½ oz butter
1 small onion (finely chopped)
1 glass Marsala, or sherry
1 dessertspoon plain flour
7½ fl oz jellied stock
1 teaspoon tomato purée
1 bayleaf
salt and pepper

For garnish
½ oz butter
½ lb tomatoes (skinned, seeds removed and sliced)
1 clove of garlic (crushed with ¼ teaspoon salt)
1½ lb spinach (freshly cooked)
5 tablespoons double cream
4-5 slices of Gruyère cheese

Method

Brown escalopes quickly on both sides in the butter, add the onion and after 1-2 minutes pour in the Marsala or sherry and flambé (set alight).

Take out veal and put on a hot plate. Boil the gravy to reduce slightly, then add the flour, stock, tomato purée, bayleaf and seasoning. Bring to the boil, put in the veal and simmer gently for 7-12 minutes.

Meanwhile prepare the garnish: melt the butter, add the tomatoes and garlic and cook briskly for 2-3 minutes.

Have the spinach ready cooked in plenty of boiling salted water. Drain well and put in a pan with the cream. Reheat and then place down centre of a long serving dish. Put the escalopes, drained from the sauce, on top and cover with the tomatoes. Arrange the sliced cheese on top and brown under the grill. Boil up the sauce and strain. Pour a little round the dish and serve the rest of it separately.

Veal chops monarque

4 veal chops
2 oz butter
4 oz mushrooms (washed and
　finely chopped)
2 oz Gruyère cheese (grated)
salt
pepper (ground from mill)
4 oz small pasta shells
¼ oz butter
2 oz ham (cut in strips)
1 wineglass port

Method

Melt 1 oz of the butter and sauté the chops slowly on one side until golden-brown; remove from pan. Put the mushrooms into the pan and cook quickly to drive off all the moisture. Reduce the heat, add the cheese and stir over gentle heat until it melts. Season to taste. Spread this mixture on the cooked side of the chops, put them back into the pan with the remaining butter and cook the undersides for 2-3 minutes.

Put the pan into oven, pre-set at 400°F or Mark 6, for 6-8 minutes to glaze the top.

Meanwhile cook the pasta in boiling water until just tender, drain and refresh, return to the pan and heat with ¼ oz butter, pepper ground from the mill and ham. Take up chops and arrange in a serving dish; pour the port into pan and bring to the boil, scraping the bottom and sides well. Strain this sauce over chops; garnish with pasta.

Veal chops monarque, with a port sauce poured over them, are garnished with a mixture of ham and small pasta shells

Escalopes of veal savoyarde

5 large veal escalopes
2 oz butter (for frying)
1 wineglass dry vermouth
1 medium-size onion (finely
   chopped)
5 slices of ham
béchamel sauce (made with ¾ oz
   butter, ½ oz flour, 7½ fl oz
   flavoured milk)
3 tablespoons double cream
salt and pepper
2 oz Gruyère cheese (grated)

For garnish
1 lb French beans
½ oz butter

Method

Brown the escalopes in a pan in
1½ oz of the butter, add the
vermouth and reduce a little.
Put escalopes and juice in an
ovenproof dish, set aside. Cook
onion for 3-4 minutes in the
pan in remaining butter, then
scatter over escalopes. Cover
each of the escalopes with a
slice of ham.
   Set oven at 375°F or Mark 5.
   Prepare béchamel sauce, stir
until boiling, then add cream.
Season well and add half the
cheese. Coat the escalopes
with sauce, sprinkle with remaining cheese. Brown the
escalopes in pre-set oven for
10-15 minutes.
   Meanwhile, cook the French
beans in boiling salted water
until tender, drain and toss in
½ oz butter. Arrange the beans
either side of the escalopes on
a serving dish.

Hungarian grenadins of veal

4 grenadins
1 aubergine
2 oz butter
1 tablespoon seasoned flour
1 shallot (finely chopped)
1 teaspoon paprika pepper
2-3 tablespoons white wine
¼ pint double cream
salt and pepper
½ pint mornay sauce
1 dessertspoon grated Parmesan
   cheese

A grenadin is a small thick 'nut'
of meat (weighing approximately 3 oz), which is cut from
the boned loin or fillet of veal.

Method

Cut the aubergine into neat
slices, score with a knife,
sprinkle lightly with salt and
leave for 30 minutes. Drain off
any liquid and wipe dry with
absorbent paper, then dust with
a little flour. Melt the butter in
a sauté pan and fry the aubergine slices for about 1 minute
on each side; remove from the
pan and keep warm. Then dust
the grenadins with the seasoned
flour and cook for about 3
minutes on each side in the
same pan, remove and keep
warm. Add the shallot to the
pan and cook it slowly for 2
minutes, then add the paprika
and continue cooking a further
2 minutes. Pour on the wine
and reduce it by half. Pour in
the cream, season, bring this
sauce to the boil and set aside.
   Place the grenadins in a
serving dish with the slices of
aubergine on the top, coat with
hot mornay sauce, sprinkle with
cheese and brown under the
grill. Reheat the paprika sauce
and pour it around the dish.

Lamb cutlets au fromage

2 lb best end of neck of lamb
  cutlets
2 oz butter (melted)
8 tablespoons fresh white
  breadcrumbs
2 oz Gruyère cheese (finely
  grated)
2 oz clarified butter, or 2
  tablespoons oil (for frying)
2 lb spinach
½ oz butter

For sauce
1 onion (finely chopped)
¾ oz butter
1 dessertspoon plain flour
1 medium-size can (½ pint)
  tomatoes
2 caps of pimiento (chopped)
pinch of ground mace
bouquet garni (containing 2
  strips of pared lemon rind)
1 teaspoon tomato purée
¼ pint stock
salt and pepper
sugar (to taste)

Method

Trim cutlets, scraping bones
well. Dip in melted butter, then
into a mixture of grated cheese
and crumbs; press this on well,
then repeat the process so that
each cutlet is covered twice.
Set cutlets aside.

To prepare sauce: cook onion
in the butter, stir in flour, then
add remaining ingredients.
Season, then simmer the sauce
for 25-30 minutes until it is
reduced. Press it through a
strainer, return it to the pan
and continue to simmer until it
is syrupy.

Cook the spinach in plenty
of boiling salted water for about
5 minutes, drain it, then press
between two plates to remove
all the water. Sauté the cutlets
in the butter or oil for 7 minutes.
Toss the spinach in the ½ oz
butter and season well. Pour a
small quantity of the sauce on
the serving dish, arrange the
cutlets in a circle and fill the
middle with the spinach.

Serve the remaining sauce
separately.

Savoury stuffed loin of lamb

3 lb loin of lamb (boned)
salt and pepper
pinch of dried marjoram
2 oz butter
2 large carrots (cut in rounds)
3 medium-size onions (peeled)
bouquet garni
1 wineglass white wine
6 oz mushrooms
4 tablespoons breadcrumbs
2 tablespoons grated Parmesan
  cheese

Method

Season the boned surface of the lamb with salt, pepper and marjoram, tie joint securely with string or fasten with poultry pins. Drop 1 oz butter in a deep flameproof casserole, put in the meat, cook quickly for 4-5 minutes on all sides (just enough to seal the meat). Reduce the heat, add the carrots, whole onions, bouquet garni, and season. Pour over the wine and cover casserole tightly. Cook very slowly on top of stove for 1 hour.

Trim and wash mushrooms, chop them finely and cook in remaining butter until all the moisture has evaporated; rub them through a sieve. Remove the onions, when cooked, from the casserole with a draining spoon, rub them through a strainer, mix with the mushroom purée and season well. Set oven at 375°F or Mark 5.

Take up the meat, which should still be pink in the centre, and carve in thick slices. Spread the purée between the slices and reshape joint in an ovenproof gratin dish, holding the meat in shape by running two skewers through the slices, one from each end. Mix the breadcrumbs and cheese together, sprinkle over the meat and season again. Brown joint lightly in pre-set moderate oven for about 20-30 minutes. Strain the juices left in the casserole, heat and pour them over the meat before serving.

Ham à la crème

2 lb middle cut of gammon
1 onion (stuck with a clove)
6 peppercorns
1 bayleaf
½ oz butter

For sauce
1½ oz butter
1½ tablespoons plain flour
1 wineglass stock
½ pint milk
salt
black pepper (ground from mill)
5 tablespoons single cream, or
    top of milk
2 tablespoons finely grated
    Gruyère, or Parmesan, cheese

Method

Cover the joint with cold water, bring slowly to the boil and then skim well. Add the onion and seasonings, cover and simmer for 1-1½ hours. Leave the gammon to stand in the liquid at least 15 minutes before removing the skin and carving.

To prepare the sauce: melt the butter, stir in the flour and then blend in the stock and milk. Season with a little salt and plenty of black pepper. Simmer the sauce gently for 15 minutes, then add the cream or milk. Stir well, add the cheese and adjust the seasoning.

Pour a little of the cream sauce into an ovenproof dish, carve the ham into even slices and arrange on top. Spoon over the rest of the sauce, then cover with ½ oz butter in shavings.

Brown ham in a hot oven at 400°F or Mark 6, for 5-10 minutes, or glaze under grill.

Meat balls (with tomato and pepper sauce)

1 lb minced raw beef
6 oz minced raw pork
1 cup (3 oz) fine dry breadcrumbs
2 oz Parmesan cheese (grated)
1 tablespoon chopped parsley
2 cloves of garlic (crushed with
    salt)
salt and pepper
2 eggs (beaten)
scant ¼ pint milk
seasoned flour
3 tablespoons dripping, or oil

For sauce
2 large onions (chopped)
1 oz plain flour
1 can (14 oz) tomatoes
2 green peppers (core and seeds
    removed, flesh chopped)
salt, pepper and sugar (to taste)
dash of Worcestershire sauce
1 bayleaf

This quantity serves 6.

Method

Mix the meat, breadcrumbs, cheese, parsley, garlic, and seasonings, and bind with the beaten eggs and milk. Shape mixture into 1½-inch balls and roll them in seasoned flour.

Melt about 3 tablespoons good dripping (or oil) in a pan and fry the meat balls a few at a time until golden-brown on all sides. Remove balls and keep warm. Add the onions to the pan and cook slowly until golden. Blend in the flour, followed by the remaining ingredients, and stir until boiling. Replace the meat balls, cover and simmer for 1 hour. Serve with plainly boiled spaghetti, tossed in butter and seasoned, allowing 2 oz pasta per person.

Chicken gratiné duxelles

3-3½ lb roasting chicken
2 pints water
1 onion
1 stick of celery
2 cardamom seeds
1-inch stick of cinnamon
salt and pepper
6 rashers back, or streaky,
    bacon
6 oz flat mushrooms (trimmed,
    washed and chopped finely)
2 oz butter
1½ oz plain flour
¾ pint milk
2 eggs (beaten)
2 tablespoons Parmesan cheese

Method

Place the chicken in a deep pan with the water and bring to the boil; skim well. Add onion, celery, spices and seasoning, cover and simmer for 2-2½ hours.

Fry the bacon until crisp, remove from frying pan and put in mushrooms, cook until dry and keep on one side.

Take up the chicken and set aside; rapidly boil the liquid in which chicken was cooked, until stock is reduced to ¼ pint. Strain and keep on one side. Place the chicken in an oven-proof gratin dish, carefully remove the skin and slice the breast meat, replacing it with the bacon between each piece. Skewer to keep in place.

To prepare sauce, melt butter in a small pan, blend in the flour, milk and reduced chicken stock and stir until boiling. Remove from the heat, add the beaten eggs, cheese and mushrooms. Spoon this duxelles-flavoured sauce over the chicken and place under the grill until golden-brown, about 7-8 minutes. Remove the skewers, but serve whole.

Chicken à la suisse

3½ lb roasting chicken
4 thin rashers of streaky bacon
1 large onion (thinly sliced)
2 large carrots (thinly sliced)
1 stick of celery (sliced)
2½ fl oz stock (made from chicken giblets)
bouquet garni
½ lb noodles
1 oz butter
pepper (ground from mill)
½ oz Parmesan cheese (grated)

For cheese sauce
1 oz butter
1 oz plain flour
¾ pint flavoured milk
2 oz Emmenthal, or Gruyère, cheese (grated)
salt and pepper
2-3 tablespoons double cream

Method

Lay the bacon on the bottom of a deep pan, cover with the onion, carrot and celery and set the trussed chicken on top. Cover the pan and cook over very gentle heat for 10-15 minutes. Pour the stock over the chicken, tuck in the herbs with the vegetables, cover again and cook gently, either on top of the stove or in the oven at 325-350°F or Mark 3-4, for about 50-60 minutes.

Meanwhile curl the noodles into a large pan of boiling salted water, reduce the heat a little and boil until just tender; drain, refresh and put back into the rinsed pan with ½ pint hand-hot water.

Prepare the sauce in the usual way, then beat in the grated Emmenthal (or Gruyère) a little at a time and taste for seasoning. Add the cream and keep the sauce warm.

Take up the chicken, reduce the gravy a little and strain. Skim off as much fat as possible, then add the liquid to the cheese sauce. Drain the noodles and heat them in the butter, adding plenty of pepper from the mill before tipping into a hot flame-proof serving dish. Carve the chicken, arrange joints on top of the noodles and coat with the sauce. Dust with the grated Parmesan and brown lightly under the grill.

The noodles for the chicken are tossed in pepper and butter

Chicken joints on noodles are coated with sauce before browning

Braised veal Orloff

2½ lb fillet of veal
1 oz butter
1 large onion (diced)
2 carrots (diced)
1 stick of celery (diced)
1 wineglass white wine
½ pint stock
salt and pepper
bouquet garni
1 rounded teaspoon arrowroot
    (mixed with 1 tablespoon cold
    water)

For soubise
2 large onions (chopped)
½ oz butter
3 oz Carolina rice
¼ pint stock
salt and pepper
1 egg yolk
1 tablespoon cream

For mornay sauce
1 oz butter
1 rounded tablespoon plain flour
½ pint milk
2-3 tablespoons grated cheese
1 tablespoon cream

To garnish
8 oz mushrooms
¼ oz butter
salt and pepper
squeeze of lemon juice

Method

Tie the veal neatly with string to keep it a good shape while cooking. Melt the butter in a flameproof casserole, add the diced vegetables and set the meat on top. Cover the dish and cook for 30 minutes in the oven at 350°F or Mark 4.

Pour over the white wine, cover the casserole again, return to the oven and continue cooking to reduce the wine (allow 30 minutes for this). Pour over the stock, which should come half-way up the meat, season, tuck in the bouquet garni by the meat and cover with greaseproof paper and the lid.

Lower the oven to 325°F or Mark 3 and cook the veal for 2 hours.

Meanwhile prepare the soubise, mornay sauce and garnish.

To prepare the soubise: cook the chopped onion gently in the butter until soft but not coloured, add the rice and stock and season. Bring to the boil, cover and cook in the oven for about 30 minutes, until very soft.

Watchpoint You must overcook rice so that each grain will split. Rub it through a wire strainer or mix to a purée in an electric blender. Then stir in the egg yolk and cream.

Trim and wash the mushrooms and cook for 1-2 minutes in ¼ oz butter, salt and pepper and a squeeze of lemon.

Take veal out of oven and keep warm. Strain the stock from the veal in the pan and thicken lightly with the arrowroot mixture. Taste for seasoning before setting aside for gravy.

Carve the meat, spread each slice with the soubise purée and reshape the joint on the serving dish. Spoon over the mornay sauce and brown in the oven at 400°F or Mark 6 for 12-15 minutes. Pour a little of the gravy round the meat and garnish with the mushrooms. Hand round gravy separately. Serve with boiled rice and Brussels sprouts.

Sauté of chicken Parmesan

2 double poussins
1 oz butter
salt and pepper
little grated rind and juice
of ½ lemon
3 tablespoons grated Parmesan
cheese
little stock, or water (optional)
1 egg yolk
2 tablespoons cream
béchamel sauce (made with
1 oz butter, 1 rounded
tablespoon plain flour, ½ pint
flavoured milk)

Method

Split the poussins in half. Melt butter in sauté pan, put in birds, skin side down, and cook slowly until golden-brown. Turn the birds, season, strain on lemon juice and add a little grated rind.

Cover pan with a close-fitting lid and cook gently for 20-30 minutes, shaking pan frequently. To keep birds moist, add a little stock or water if the pan gets dry.

Remove birds, trim away backbone, set in serving dish and keep warm. Make béchamel sauce, pour in pan. Boil up well, then strain. Add 2 tablespoons of cheese to sauce, reheat carefully, then taste for seasoning. Work egg yolk and cream together in a bowl, mix with a little hot sauce, then pour slowly back in pan; reheat without boiling and spoon over chicken. Sprinkle with remaining cheese and brown in a hot oven at 400°F or Mark 6, or under the grill.

Roast fillet of beef Dubarry

2½-3 lb fillet of beef
piece of pork fat, or unsmoked
bacon fat, or beef fat (for barding)
2-3 tablespoons oil, or beef dripping

For gravy
1 dessertspoon plain flour
½-¾ pint beef stock
salt and pepper

For garnish
1 large cauliflower
little grated cheese

For thick mornay sauce
1 oz butter
2 tablespoons plain flour
1 pint milk
2 oz grated cheese

Method

The garnish can be prepared ahead of time. Break the cauliflower into sprigs and cook until just tender in boiling, salted water (about 5 minutes). Drain and refresh by pouring over cold water. Press 1-2 cauliflower sprigs at a time in muslin to form balls and set them on a buttered baking sheet. Have ready the mornay sauce and coat the tiny cauliflower sprigs with this. Sprinkle with a little extra grated cheese and keep on one side.

Set oven at 400°F or Mark 7.

Bard (wrap fat round) meat and tie at regular intervals with fine string. The pork fat protects the very lean meat and keeps it moist during cooking. If you do not like the flavour of pork or bacon fat, put an extra piece of beef fat on top of the meat after it has been tied with string. The string keeps the meat in good shape while cooking; without it small pieces of fillet curl when first basted and put in oven.

Baste the meat well with hot oil or dripping and put to roast on the grill pan grid, or a wire cake rack, in the roasting tin. Baste every 15 minutes and turn when half cooked. For a 2 lb joint allow 15 minutes per lb and 15 minutes over; for a 3 lb or larger piece, allow 15 minutes per lb with no extra time. Bake the cauliflower sprigs on the top shelf of the oven for 10-15 minutes while it is still at a roasting temperature.

Take cooked meat from oven, remove string and barding fat; keep the joint warm. Tilt the roasting tin gently and pour off the fat, take care to leave the sediment and juices undisturbed in the corner of the pan (to do this successfully use a spoon for the last of the dripping).

Dust pan very lightly with the flour, work this into the sediment and scrape down the sides of the pan. Cook over a gentle heat until well coloured. Draw aside and blend in the stock. Stir gravy until boiling, season, and then boil hard until well-reduced and strong in flavour. Strain into a gravy boat.

Just before serving, carve the meat in the kitchen and put back on hot serving dish, spooning any juice that runs out over meat.

Watchpoint Never add these juices to the gravy as they would coagulate and spoil its appearance.

Arrange the small cauliflower sprigs around the dish.

Swiss cheese fondue

10-12 oz Swiss Emmenthal
10-12 oz Swiss Gruyère
1 clove of garlic (cut)
½ oz flour
2 wineglasses dry white wine
1 teaspoon lemon juice
1½ fl oz kirsch
grated nutmeg
black pepper (ground from mill)
French bread (for serving)

Method

Rub inside of pan with garlic. Grate cheeses and mix with flour, put into pan and add wine and lemon juice. Bring to boil over a moderate heat, stirring continuously in a figure of eight. Add kirsch, season with nutmeg and pepper, and bring back to boil. The fondue should be of a creamy consistency and is now ready to serve. Keep simmering throughout meal. Serve with French bread (retaining crust), cut into cubes.

A pot of bubbling Swiss fondue —a delicious centrepiece for a cheese and wine party

Fondue Cordon Bleu

6 eggs (beaten)
4 oz butter
4 oz Gruyère cheese (grated)
4 oz Cheddar cheese (grated)
2 oz Parmesan cheese (freshly grated)
3-4 tablespoons dry white wine, or double cream
salt and pepper
toast or French bread (for serving)

Method

Beat eggs well with a fork. Pour into a fondue pot or chafing dish set over a spirit lamp or a very low heat. When eggs are beginning to set, add the butter in small pieces and, when melted, the cheese and wine or cream. Season, and stir until thickened and creamy.

Serve as for Swiss fondue.

Watchpoint The reason for mixing the cheeses is that with Gruyère cheese alone a fondue quickly becomes stringy unless care is taken. Parmesan also adds a distinctive flavour.

Scalloped crab

1 large crab, or 1 large can crab claw meat
¾ pint béchamel sauce
3-4 sticks celery (finely sliced)
salt and pepper
4 tablespoons breadcrumbs
2 tablespoons grated Cheddar cheese
1 oz butter

Method

Have the crab ready picked and the béchamel sauce prepared. Set oven at 350°F or Mark 4.

Mix the sliced celery with the crab meat and sauce and season to taste. Tip the mixture into a buttered gratin dish, cover with the breadcrumbs and cheese, dot with the butter and bake in the pre-set moderate oven for 20 minutes or until hot, and brown on top.

Sweet cheese dishes

Bring change into the menu with a sweet cheese dish. Whether you make your own curd cheese from the directions on page 11, or whether you buy it from your local delicatessen, you can delight the family with some of these cakes and tarts. Many are traditional regional specialities that have been made for centuries on farms where there is an ample supply of milk for cheese.

Sweetened with sugar or mixed with fruit, cheese is as rich as cream, and far more unusual. Make cheesecake a regular treat in your family, as it is in many Jewish homes, or surprise guests with a delicious cream cheese strudel—better than anything you could buy.

Beauceronne tart

For rich shortcrust pastry
6 oz plain flour
pinch of salt
4½ oz butter
1 egg yolk
1 rounded dessertspoon sugar
2 tablespoons cold water
whipped cream (optional)

For filling
8 oz curd cheese
2 oz butter
2 rounded tablespoons caster
    sugar
2 rounded tablespoons raisins
2 tablespoons double cream
3 eggs (separated)
2 level tablespoons plain flour

8-inch diameter flan ring, or sand-
   wich tin

Method

Make the rich shortcrust pastry and set aside to chill. Line the pastry on to the flan ring.

Now sieve the cheese and work well in a warm bowl. This will help the cheese to absorb the butter, sugar, cream and yolks without curdling, and allow the whisked egg whites to be folded in easily.

Cream the butter with the sugar in a bowl and beat well. Stir in the raisins, cream and egg yolks. When well mixed, whip egg whites stiffly and, using a metal spoon, fold into the mixture with the flour.

Turn into the pastry case and bake for 35-40 minutes in an oven at 375-400°F or Mark 5-6. When cooked leave to cool as the filling rises a lot during cooking and must be left to subside before attempting to remove the flan ring or turn the tart out of the tin.

Serve cold and, for a special occasion, with lightly whipped cream.

Cheese blintzes

For batter
4 oz plain flour
pinch of salt
1 egg
1 egg yolk
1 teaspoon oil
½ pint milk

For filling
8 oz curd, or cream, cheese
1 egg
salt
sugar to taste
grated rind of ½ lemon

Method

To prepare the batter: sift the flour with a pinch of salt into a deep basin. Make a well in the flour and drop in the egg, yolk and oil. Mix with a wooden spoon, slowly drawing in the flour and adding milk as needed to keep the mixture at the consistency of unwhipped cream. When all the flour is combined half the milk should have been used. Now beat for 1 minute. Stir in the remaining milk. Cover batter and keep in a cool place for 30-60 minutes.

Meanwhile, beat the cheese to soften it lightly and combine all ingredients for the filling. Fry thin pancakes in a hot, oiled pan (on one side only). Place pancakes on a clean cloth, cooked side uppermost, and place 1 tablespoon of the filling on each one. Roll up like a parcel and fry until golden on all sides.

Cheesecake 1

2½ oz butter
5 oz caster sugar
10 oz curd cheese
2 eggs (separated)
2 oz ground almonds
2 oz raisins
2 tablespoons semolina
rind and juice of 1 lemon

*7-8 inch diameter shallow cake tin,
or sandwich tin*

This recipe makes a good sized cake which may be served with a hot fruit sauce as a sweet.

Method

Set oven at 350°F or Mark 4. Line the cake tin with greased greaseproof paper.

Cream the butter and sugar, add curd cheese gradually and cream well, then slowly add the egg yolks. Beat thoroughly and, when very creamy, add the almonds, raisins, semolina, lemon and stiffly whisked egg whites.

Pour mixture into greased tin and bake in pre-set moderate oven for 45-60 minutes. Then turn it out on to a plate.

Cheesecake 2

For pastry
6 oz plain flour
4 oz butter
3 oz sugar
2 egg yolks
grated rind and juice of ½ lemon

For filling
3 oz butter
3 oz sugar
3 eggs (separated)
14 oz curd cheese
2-3 drops of vanilla essence, or
grated rind of ½ lemon

*Deep 7-8 inch diameter sandwich
tin, or Yorkshire pudding tin*

This is a rich cheesecake and the quantities above make a large one; they may, of course, be halved.

Method

Sift the flour on to a board and make a well in the centre. In this put the butter, sugar, egg yolks and flavouring. Work with the fingers of one hand to a firm paste. Leave for 30 minutes. Set oven at 375°F or Mark 5. Roll out the pastry and line it on to the bottom of the chosen tin. Prick base and bake to a pale golden-brown in the pre-set oven for 40-45 minutes. Allow pastry to cool.

Cream the butter, then work in the sugar, egg yolks and curd cheese. Flavour to taste with vanilla essence (or lemon rind). Lastly mix in the stiffly whipped egg whites. Spread this mixture on the pastry about 1-1½ inches thick. Return to the oven, lower the heat to 350°F or Mark 4 and bake for 30-35 minutes. Cool a little before turning out.

Cheesecake 3

For rich shortcrust pastry
6 oz plain flour
4 oz butter
1 egg yolk
2-3 tablespoons water

For filling
½ lb curd cheese
1¾ oz butter
1¾ oz sugar
1 oz plain flour
handful of raisins (stoned)
2 tablespoons double cream
3 eggs (separated)

7-8 inch diameter sandwich tin, or flan ring

Method

Set oven at 375-400°F or Mark 5-6. Make pastry and line on to tin or ring. Sieve cheese. Cream butter, add sugar and beat well. Work in flour, raisins, cream, egg yolks and cheese. When well mixed, fold in stiffly whipped egg whites. Turn into pastry case and bake in pre-set oven for 40-45 minutes. Remove ring or turn out of tin when cool.

Kosher cheesecake

**6 oz quantity of shortcrust pastry,
   or 4-6 oz biscuit crumbs mixed
   with 1-2 oz melted butter
3 eggs
8 oz caster sugar
1½ lb curd cheese
2 oz plain flour
¼ pint double cream
pinch of salt
grated rind and juice of 1 lemon**

*7-8 inch loose bottom, or spring
form, cake tin*

Method

Line a greased baking tin with
the shortcrust pastry or prepared
crumbs. Set the oven at 350°F
or Mark 4.

Place the eggs and sugar in a
bowl and beat until light and
creamy. In another bowl,
thoroughly beat the cheese
and flour; add cream, salt,
lemon juice and rind. Combine
the mixtures and again beat
well.

Pour the mixture into lined tin
and bake in the pre-set oven
for 1¼ hours. Then turn off the
oven and open the door slightly.

Take the cake out after 20
minutes. This keeps the cake,
which rises in baking, from
relaxing too quickly and thus
becoming stodgy. This cake is
best left overnight before cutting.

Viennese curd cake

**about 6 oz semi-sweet biscuits
1½ oz butter
4½ oz sugar
12 oz curd cheese
3 egg whites
scant ½ oz gelatine (soaked and
   dissolved in 2 tablespoons
   water)
2-3 drops of vanilla essence
7½ fl oz double cream (lightly
   whipped)**

8-inch diameter flan ring

Method

Butter the inside of the flan
ring. Crush biscuits, melt butter
and stir in the biscuit crumbs
with 1 oz of the sugar. Put half
of this mixture at the bottom of
the flan ring. Cream the curd
cheese and the remaining sugar
together, whisk the egg whites
until stiff. Beat dissolved gelatine into curd and sugar mixture,
add vanilla essence. Fold in
cream and egg whites. Pour
into flan ring, smooth the top
and cover with rest of the
crumbs. Leave to set.

Maids of honour

8 oz quantity of rough puff, or puff, pastry

For filling
2½ pints milk and 1 tablespoon rennet, or 4-5 oz curd cheese
1 egg (beaten)
1 oz butter (melted)
2 oz caster sugar
grated rind and juice of ½ lemon

12-18 2¼-inch diameter patty tins; 3-inch diameter plain cutter

Method

Make the pastry and then prepare the filling. Warm the milk to blood heat, add the rennet and leave for 2½ hours. Squeeze the curd gently in butter muslin to remove excess whey or, if using curd cheese, sieve it; then add the egg, butter, sugar, lemon rind and juice.

Set oven at 400°F or Mark 6. Roll out the pastry to ½-inch thickness, stamp out rounds with the cutter and line them on to patty tins. Press the pastry at the bottom of the tins with the thumbs and lightly prick with a fork. Fill with the curd mixture and bake for about 30 minutes in the pre-set hot oven.

Cream cheese strudel 1

For pastry
6-8 oz plain flour
pinch of salt
1 small egg
1 dessertspoon oil
½ cup warm water
melted butter
2-3 tablespoons browned crumbs

For filling
12 oz curd cheese (sieved)
2 oz butter (creamed)
2 oz caster sugar
2½ oz sultanas, or raisins (soaked in water for 2-3 hours)
grated rind of 1 lemon
juice of ½ lemon
2 teaspoons plain flour
2 egg yolks, or 1 egg (beaten)

Method

To make pastry: sieve the flour with a pinch of salt. Beat the egg, add the oil and warm water to it. Pour this liquid into the flour and beat until you have a soft, elastic dough. Leave it in a covered bowl in a warm place for 10-15 minutes. Roll out the dough to ¼-inch thickness. Lift it on to floured cloth and leave for 7-10 minutes.

Set oven at 400°F or Mark 6.

To prepare the filling: work the creamed butter with the sugar, beat in the curd gradually. Add the well-drained sultanas (or raisins), lemon rind and juice, flour and egg.

Now pull the paste gently from the edges until it is paper thin (you should be able to read through it).

Using a brush, dab the dough with melted butter, scatter over browned crumbs, then dot with the filling. Roll it up carefully. Then, tilting the cloth, tip the strudel on to a greased baking sheet and bake in the pre-set hot oven for 20-30 minutes. Dust well with icing sugar, cut in slices and serve with a cherry compote.

Cream cheese strudel is served in slices with cherry compote

Cream cheese strudel 2

strudel pastry (as for cream cheese strudel 1)

For filling
8 oz curd cheese
1 oz caster sugar
1 egg
little grated lemon rind
2 oz browned hazel nuts

Method

Prepare the strudel pastry and roll out as for previous recipe. Cream the cheese with the sugar, beat in the egg and add a little lemon rind. Chop the hazelnuts and add to the mixture. Finish the strudel and serve as in the previous recipe.

Crème suisse

4 eggs (separated)
2-3 oz caster sugar
6 Petit Suisse, or the equivalent in cream cheese (approximately 6 oz)
¼ pint double cream
½ liqueur glass Grand Marnier

To serve
sugared raspberries, or raspberries in Melba sauce

Method

Cream the egg yolks with the sugar and work in the cream cheese, cream and Grand Marnier. Whip the egg whites stiffly and fold them into the mixture. Put the cream into the freezing compartment of the refrigerator or turn into an ice cube tray and chill thoroughly for 2 hours.

Spoon cream into a chilled bowl and serve with sugared raspberries.

Apricot curd cake

½ lb apricots (stoned)
sugar syrup (made with ⅓ pint water and 2 tablespoons granulated sugar)
6 oz sweet biscuits (eg. Nice)
2 oz butter
1 lb curd cheese
4 oz caster sugar
1 large, or 2 small, eggs (well beaten)
2-3 drops of vanilla essence
cream (lightly whipped)

7-inch diameter loose-bottomed flan ring, or sandwich tin

Method

Set oven at 350°F or Mark 4. Make sugar syrup and poach apricots in it. Crush biscuits with a rolling pin; rub ½ oz butter over bottom and sides of the flan tin.

Rub the curd cheese through a wire strainer. Cream rest of butter, add sugar and cheese by degrees with the egg and beat until light and fluffy; flavour with vanilla essence. Scatter half biscuit crumbs over bottom and sides of tin, then carefully spoon in curd mixture. Smooth top with a palette knife, scatter over remaining crumbs. Bake in pre-set oven 25-30 minutes.

Leave overnight, or at least 4 hours, before removing from tin. Drain apricots, arrange over top of cake; boil syrup until thick, spoon over apricots. Serve with whipped cream.

Pineapple curd cake

For pastry
4 oz plain flour
pinch of salt
2 oz butter
½ oz shortening
1 teaspoon sugar
1 tablespoon distilled white
 vinegar
1 tablespoon milk

For filling
1 small pineapple, or ½ a large one
8 oz Philadelphia, or curd, cheese
2 tablespoons sugar
2 egg yolks
¼ pint double cream

7-8 inch diameter flan ring

Method

Prepare the pastry. Sift flour with salt and sugar, rub in fats, and mix to a firm dough with the vinegar and milk. Roll out to a round the same diameter as the flan ring, and fit the pastry into the ring's base. Prick lightly and set aside.

Set the oven at 375°F or Mark 5.

Beat the cheese until smooth, add the sugar, egg yolks and cream. Turn the mixture into the ring and bake in the pre-set oven for 20-30 minutes until firm to the touch.

In the meantime, cut the skin from the pineapple, cut flesh into slices and core them, dust slices with sugar. When curd cake is cooked, leave it until cold, and then arrange the pineapple on top, slightly overlapping the slices. Serve with a bowl of lightly whipped cream.

Mixing sugar, egg yolks and cream into the smooth cheese

Overlapping fresh pineapple slices on top of cooled cake

Swiss pancakes à la crème

8 drop scones (see recipe page
122, omitting peppers and
cheese), or 4 large Scotch
pancakes
3 oz cream cheese
1 teaspoon caster sugar
2-3 drops of vanilla essence
1 small carton (2½ fl oz) double
cream
1 tablespoon black cherry, or
bilberry, jam

Method

Mix cream cheese with sugar,
vanilla and half the cream. Put
a teaspoon of this on four
scones or on each pancake. Put
a second drop scone on the top
of the cream cheese, or roll the
pancake up like a fat cigar.
Spoon over the remaining cream
and glaze the top under a hot
grill. Serve with a teaspoon of
hot or cold jam on the top.

Tartelettes coeur à la crème

For French flan pastry
4 oz plain flour
2 oz butter
2 oz caster sugar
2 egg yolks
2 drops of vanilla essence

For filling
4 oz Petit Suisse, or Demi-Sel,
cream cheese
caster sugar (to taste)
2-3 tablespoons double cream
½ lb small ripe strawberries
(hulled)
½ lb redcurrant jelly

6-8 tartlet tins

Method

Prepare the flan pastry and chill
for 1 hour before rolling out.
Set oven at 375°F or Mark 5.
Line tartlet tins with the pastry,
prick the bottoms with a fork
and bake them blind in pre-set
oven for 8-10 minutes.
    Rub the cream cheese through
a small sieve, add sugar to taste
and beat in the cream.
    When the pastry cases are
cold, fill with the cheese-cream
mixture and cover with the
strawberries. Make a glaze from
the redcurrant jelly by whisking
until fairly smooth and rubbing
it through a strainer into a pan.
Heat gently without stirring
until it is clear, then bring to the
boil and brush the warm glaze
over the strawberries. Allow to
set before serving.

Party savouries

Party time is the important time. When you have lots of guests and your time is limited, the choice of food is critical to the success of the occasion. With cheese you will be able to provide just what is required in the way of savouries. Snacks that can be prepared in advance and heated up at the last minute will save you time and if your guests can eat them without cutlery they will be very grateful for the convenience—not to mention the delicious variety of savouries you can provide.

Liptauer cheese

4 oz curd, or cottage, cheese
4 oz butter
1 dessertspoon chopped chives
1 dessertspoon caraway seeds
1 dessertspoon paprika pepper
1 dessertspoon chopped capers
2 fillets of anchovy (finely
   chopped)
1 teaspoon made English mustard
½ teaspoon salt
pinch of celery salt

This is a highly flavoured cheese, suitable for eating in small quantities as in cocktail savouries. It keeps well for several days in a covered jar.

Method
Sieve the cheese. Cream the butter and beat in the cheese gradually. Add the remaining ingredients and mix thoroughly. Pile up in a dish to serve.

Cheese profiteroles

For choux pastry
¼ pint water
2 oz butter, or margarine
2½ oz plain flour
2 eggs

2¼ oz Parmesan cheese (grated)
salt and pepper
cayenne pepper
dry mustard
a little beaten egg

Method
Set oven at 400°F or Mark 6. Make choux pastry (see method, page 108). Season and add 2 oz Parmesan cheese. Put mixture out with a teaspoon on to a dampened baking sheet. Brush lightly with beaten egg and sprinkle with remaining Parmesan cheese. Bake on a rising temperature for 20-30 minutes until golden-brown and crisp. Serve the profiteroles hot.

Celery pinwheels

1 good head of celery
1 oz butter
1 Demi-Sel cheese
4 oz Dolcelatte, or cream, cheese
brown bread and butter
pimiento (to garnish)

Method
Divide the celery into sticks, wash thoroughly and dry.

Soften butter, work in Demi-Sel and Dolcelatte, beat until smooth. Fill each stick with cheese mixture and, starting with the smallest pieces, reshape celery head. Wrap in grease-proof paper; chill before slicing.

Cut bread and butter into rounds the same diameter as the celery slices. Place the celery on the bread and garnish with a round of pimiento.

Savoury petits choux

¼ pint water
2 oz butter
2½ oz plain flour
salt and pepper
pinch of cayenne pepper
2 eggs
little beaten egg
little Parmesan cheese (grated)

Forcing bag and vegetable pipe

These petits choux should be filled — at the last possible moment — with one of the three fillings which follow this recipe. This quantity will make about 18 petits choux.

Method
Put water and butter into a fairly large pan. Sift flour and seasoning on to a piece of paper. Bring contents of pan to the boil; when bubbling draw pan aside and pour in all the flour. Stir vigorously until smooth.

Cool mixture for about 5 minutes, then beat in eggs, one at a time. Beat pastry for about 3 minutes until it looks glossy. Set the oven at 400°F or Mark 6. Using the vegetable pipe, pipe out the mixture into very small balls on to a dampened baking sheet. Brush the top of each ball with a little beaten egg and dust with Parmesan cheese.

Bake in the pre-set oven for about 12 minutes, or until very crisp to the touch. Remove from oven and leave to cool.

Filling 1

1 oz cream cheese
1 tablespoon chopped celery
1 tablespoon chopped green
  pepper (blanched and
  drained)
1 teaspoon chopped chives
1 teaspoon tomato ketchup
salt and pepper
little cream (optional)

Method
Work all the ingredients together and season well, adding a little cream if necessary to make a good consistency.

Filling 2

1 oz cream cheese
salt and pepper
squeeze of lemon juice
1 tablespoon cream
2 oz potted shrimps

Method
Work the cream cheese with the seasoning, lemon juice and cream, add potted shrimps.

Filling 3

2-3 oz cooked chicken
  trimmings (finely diced)
1 tablespoon thick mayonnaise
1 oz cooked tongue (chopped) —
  optional

Method
Bind the chicken with the mayonnaise. Add the tongue, if wished, to give extra flavour.

Cheese beignets

¼ pint water
2 oz butter, or margarine
2½ oz plain flour
2 eggs
2 oz Parmesan, or dry Cheddar,
  cheese (grated)

For serving
little extra Parmesan cheese
cayenne pepper

Method

Prepare the choux pastry as for savoury petits choux (left), mixing in 2 oz cheese before frying. Divide the pastry out into heaped teaspoons on a tin or dish.

Heat a deep fat bath to 370°F, dip a palette knife in the fat and use this to lift each teaspoon of pastry into the fat. Leave plenty of room for beignets to swell.

Once the beignets begin to puff out, increase heat gradually and continue cooking for about 8 minutes until they are golden-brown and firm to the touch.

Lift out, drain on absorbent paper and dust with Parmesan cheese and cayenne.

The finished beignets, dusted with Parmesan cheese and cayenne

Cheese rolls

1 sliced loaf (thinly cut)
about 4 oz cheese (grated)
4 oz butter (melted)
paprika pepper

The flavour of the cheese is improved if a little Parmesan is included.

Method
Set oven at 400°F or Mark 6. Remove crusts from bread and flatten each slice by rolling very firmly with a rolling pin. Brush with a little of the butter, dust with cheese and paprika and roll up.

Put rolls in a baking tray and brush well with more butter. Bake about 10 minutes, then turn over, brush with remaining butter, and continue cooking until really crisp and golden-brown. Serve hot.

Cheese dip

Cheddar cheese (grated)
an equal volume of butter
anchovy essence (to taste)
Worcestershire sauce (to taste)
chopped capers
chopped gherkins
chopped olives
sweet pickle
chives
crushed garlic
salt
pepper (ground from mill)
paprika pepper

To serve
potato crisps
salty biscuits
olives
radishes
gherkins

Hot milk, cream or yoghourt, or a mixture of all three, may be added in place of some or all the butter. Curd cheese may also be added.

Method
Pound or sieve the cheese and beat it well with the butter and other ingredients (its consistency should be that of cream). Taste for seasoning and flavouring, pile on to a dish and surround with the serving ingredients.

Cheese dreams

2 oz Cheddar cheese (grated)
2½ oz cream cheese
½ teaspoon paprika pepper
1 small clove of garlic (crushed)
pinch of mace
pinch of caraway
pepper (ground from mill)
2 shallots (finely sliced)
butter (for frying)
4 slices of stale bread

Serve with salads.

Method

Cream the butter with the cheeses and beat well, adding the seasonings. Fry the shallots in a little butter until soft, and fold into the mixture with a wooden spoon. Spread the mixture thickly over 2 slices of bread and sandwich them with the other slices. Cut in half and fry in butter.

Cheese marbles

½ pint grated Cheddar cheese
½ tablespoon plain flour
salt and pepper
pinch of cayenne pepper
2 egg whites
1 egg yolk
dry white breadcrumbs
browned almonds (chopped) —
    optional

Serve with salads.

Method

Mix the flour, cheese and seasoning. Beat the egg whites until stiff, add to the mixture to bind, and shape the mixture into marble-size pieces. Add the almonds to breadcrumbs, coat the marbles with egg and crumbs and fry in deep fat until golden-brown.

Cheese loaves

1 small white sandwich loaf
1 small brown sandwich loaf
1¼ lb mild Cheddar cheese
    (finely grated)
little boiling milk
6 oz unsalted butter (softened)
salt and pepper
1 bunch of watercress (finely
    chopped)
4-6 eggs (hard-boiled and
    chopped)
6 oz cooked ham (finely
    chopped or minced)
2-3 tablespoons tomato chutney
chopped radishes, olives,
    gherkins and small cress

Forcing bag and vegetable rose pipe

Use loaves that are one day old.

Method
Remove the crusts from both loaves and cut each one lengthways, to give four brown and six white slices. Add a little boiling milk to the grated cheese and beat well to a smooth cream. Work 4 oz of the butter into the cheese. Season and set aside two-thirds of the mixture. Divide the remaining third into two portions, add the finely chopped watercress to one, and the chopped egg to the other, set aside.

Work the ham to a paste with the tomato chutney, adding the remaining softened butter to bind the mixture.

To make two cheese loaves: take two slices of the white bread and cover each with a layer of the watercress mixture. Continue with a layer of brown bread for each loaf, spread with the ham filling; then a further layer of white bread spread with egg mixture, cover the egg with brown bread. Make the last layer watercress and cover with a slice of white bread.

Press each loaf well, leave a board and weight on the top and chill slightly until firm. Then spread the top and sides of the loaves with the plain cheese. Smooth with a palette knife, and pipe a little of the cheese to decorate the top, or decorate top as desired.

Garnish loaves with radishes, olives and gherkins, and arrange the small cress around the edges. Chill the loaves again and then cut into thin slices for serving.

1 *Spreading the ham and tomato mixture on a brown bread layer*
2 *Piping the cheese mixture to decorate the top edges of loaf*

Open crispbread sandwiches

Choose a selection of these for your party. Each of the toppings is sufficient for 6-8 pieces of crispbread. Use dark rye crispbread and keep the sandwiches covered until serving.

Herring and Demi-Sel topping

1 fillet of herring (preserved in white wine)
1 packet (about 2 oz) Demi-Sel cream cheese
1½ oz unsalted butter
black pepper (ground from mill)

These herring fillets can be bought at most provision counters or delicatessens. They are large and fat, so one is plenty for 6-7 pieces of crispbread.

Method
Work the Demi-Sel and butter together to a cream. Spread it fairly thickly on the pieces of crispbread. Dab the fillet dry with a paper towel to remove any surplus dressing and cut it into thin strips. Lay these lattice-fashion over the cheese and grind a little black pepper over the top.

Cheese and chutney topping

6-8 wafer-thin slices of Gouda, or Gruyère, cheese
1 tablespoon sweet spiced chutney
2 oz butter (creamed)
black pepper (ground from mill)

Method
Work the butter with chutney, seasoning well with black pepper; spread this on the pieces of crispbread and cover with the cheese.

Ham and cream cheese topping

4 oz thinly sliced smoked, or fresh, ham
1 packet (3 oz) Philadelphia cream cheese
1 oz butter
French, or German, mustard
watercress (to garnish)

Method
Work the cheese and butter together, flavouring lightly with mustard. Spread this mixture on the pieces of crispbread. Cut the slices of ham in half and lay two slices on each piece of crispbread. Serve with a little crisp watercress in the centre of the plate.

Open crispbread sandwiches are popular for an informal lunch gathering or a coffee party, as guests need no knives or forks

Party sandwiches

Ham and cream cheese sandwich

Take dark rye bread, butter and spread with a very thin layer of English mustard. Then spread with a ¼-inch layer of cream cheese, well seasoned with celery salt. Cover this with 2-3 layers of sliced ham and then with a second slice of buttered bread.

Cream cheese and pineapple sandwich

Butter wholemeal bread and cover each slice with a ½-inch layer of cream cheese and cover the bottom slice with chopped watercress. Place a slice of fresh pineapple, cut into bite-size pieces, on top of watercress and top with second slice of bread and cheese.

Mortadella open sandwich

Spread thinly sliced pumpernickel with unsalted butter, cover with finely sliced Dutch cheese such as Edam or Samso. Cover the cheese with sliced mortadella and serve open with a garnish of sliced stuffed olive.

Cheese palmiers

6 oz puff pastry, or trimmings
Parmesan cheese (grated)

Method

Roll out the pastry to a strip, sprinkle liberally with half the cheese, fold in three and roll out. Repeat this once more. Rest the pastry for at least 30 minutes.

Set oven at 425°F or Mark 7. Then roll out pastry to a square, fold one side twice towards the centre, fold the opposite side the same way. Turn one fold on top of the other and press firmly. Cut into pieces across the folds a good ¼-inch wide.

Place palmiers cut side down on a baking sheet, press each one with the 'heel' of the hand to flatten. Bake in pre-set oven. When brown on one side, turn and complete the cooking on the other side (about 15-20 minutes).

Potted cheese

6 oz mixed cheeses (free from
   rind), including a little blue
   cheese (eg. Gorgonzola)
3 oz butter
salt and pepper
2-3 tablespoons port, or sherry

Small china, or earthenware, pots

Method

Make as for cheese cream (page
22). Season well and substitute
port or sherry for milk and herbs.
The mixture should be stiffer
than cheese cream. Press into
the small pots and smooth over
the top. If not for immediate use,
cover with a round of foil and a
lid, if possible. Store in a cool
place. It will keep for 2-3 weeks.
   Either serve in the pots or
turn out and cut in slices.

Feuilletées

8 oz puff pastry
10-12 oz Roquefort cheese
1 egg (beaten)

Method

Set oven at 425°F or Mark 7.
Roll out the pastry to a piece
about 12-14 inches long and
8 inches wide.
   Cut the Roquefort into eight
'fingers' about 3 inches long,
brush half of the pastry with
water and lay the cheese on
this at intervals. Cover with the
other half of the pastry, pressing
it down well between each
piece of cheese. Cut out the
'fingers' and brush lightly with
beaten egg.
   Bake in pre-set oven for
15-20 minutes. Serve hot.

Austrian cheese cakes

6 oz plain flour
4 oz butter
2 oz ground almonds
3 oz dry Cheddar cheese (grated)
salt and pepper
1 egg yolk
1 dessertspoon water (optional)
beaten egg
Parmesan cheese (for sprinkling)

For filling
1½ oz grated cheese
¼ pint milk
1 teaspoon arrowroot
salt and pepper
1 teaspoon paprika pepper
1 egg (separated)

1-1½ inch diameter plain cutter

Method

Sift flour, rub in butter very
lightly. Add almonds, cheese
and seasoning. Bind with egg
yolk and water if necessary.
Chill for 15 minutes.
   Set oven at 375°F or Mark 5.
Roll out to about ⅛ inch thick
and stamp into rounds about
1-1½ inches in diameter. Brush
half of these with beaten egg
and sprinkle with Parmesan
cheese. Place on baking sheets
lined with greaseproof paper
and bake in pre-set oven for
10-12 minutes until golden-
brown. Allow to cool.
   Meanwhile prepare filling: mix
all the ingredients together
adding the egg yolk and reserving the white. Bring slowly to
the boil, stirring all the time.
When at boiling point, draw
aside. Whisk white to a firm
snow and fold gently into the
hot mixture. Bring again to the
boil and turn out to cool.
   Sandwich the rounds together
with a good teaspoon of the
filling, using the plain round as
the base.

Cheese straws

4 oz plain flour
3 oz butter, or luxury margarine
2 oz dry cheese (grated)
1 egg yolk

Method

Set oven at 375°F or Mark 5. Mix ingredients into a rich shortcrust pastry; chill before rolling out about ¼ inch thick. Cut into even strips about ¼ inch wide and 4 inches long. Shape 6 of these strips into rings, leave the rest as they are. Bake on baking sheets lined with greaseproof paper in pre-set oven for about 10 minutes or until golden-brown.

When cold, lift the straws off paper and slip 4-5 into each ring. Arrange carefully on serving dishes as cheese straws are fragile.

Cheese sablés

3 oz cheese (grated)
3 oz plain flour (sifted)
3 oz butter
salt and pepper
1 egg (lightly beaten)

Method

Sift flour into a bowl. Cut butter into flour with a palette knife and, as soon as pieces are well coated with flour, rub in with your fingertips until mixture resembles fine breadcrumbs.

Add cheese and season to taste. Press mixture together to make a dough. Flour, wrap dough in greaseproof paper, chill in refrigerator. Set oven at 375°F or Mark 5.

Carefully roll out pastry into a fairly thin oblong, flouring rolling pin well because this pastry tends to stick; if it does, ease it free with a palette knife. Cut into strips about 2 inches wide. Brush with beaten egg and cut strips into triangles.

Place sablés on a baking sheet lined with greaseproof paper, and cook in the pre-set oven for 10 minutes until golden-brown.

Watchpoint Take baking sheet out of oven at once. Lift off greaseproof paper, with cooked sablés on it. Cheese scorches easily so that if you remove them from oven one by one, the last biscuits could become scorched through over-cooking.

Serve the sablés cold.

Almond sablés

For pastry
6 oz plain flour
4 oz butter
1½ oz ground almonds
3 oz Cheddar cheese (grated)
salt and pepper
½ teaspoon paprika pepper
1 egg yolk
1 tablespoon water
1 egg (lightly beaten)

For filling
1 teaspoon arrowroot, or
  cornflour
1 egg (separated)
1 teaspoon paprika pepper
salt and pepper
5 fl oz milk (warmed)
1½ oz cheese (grated)

Method

Sift the flour into a bowl. Cut butter into flour with a palette knife and, as soon as the pieces are well coated with flour, rub in with your fingertips until the mixture resembles breadcrumbs. Mix in the almonds, cheese and seasonings. Beat the egg yolk, adding half the water. Pour into the bowl and mix to a dough, adding the remaining water if necessary. Lightly flour the dough, wrap it in greaseproof paper and chill it in the refrigerator for 15 minutes. Set the oven at 375°F or Mark 5.

Roll out the dough ⅛-¼ inch thick, and stamp out rounds with pastry cutter; brush half the rounds with beaten egg. Place sablés on a baking sheet lined with greaseproof paper and bake in the pre-set oven for about 10 minutes or until golden-brown. Cool slightly.

Meanwhile prepare the filling. Put the arrowroot (or cornflour), egg yolk, paprika, salt and pepper into a pan, mix and add the milk and cheese slowly. When blended place the pan over moderate heat and bring to the boil, stirring; draw aside. Whip the egg white to a firm snow and fold into the sauce. Return to heat and cook for a minute or two, stirring slowly.

Place a teaspoon of filling on the unbrushed sablés, and sandwich with brushed ones, keeping the brushed sides on top.

Note: If serving as an after-dinner savoury, rather than for cocktails, half the above quantity will be enough for 4 people. However, the sablés keep well in an airtight tin, and the filling may be kept in the refrigerator.

Roquefort tartlets

For rich shortcrust pastry
6 oz plain flour
pinch of salt
4 oz butter
1 egg yolk
1-2 tablespoons cold water

For filling
¼ pint double cream
¼ pint béchamel sauce (made with
   ½ oz butter, 1 tablespoon flour,
   ¼ pint flavoured milk)
4 oz Roquefort cheese (grated)
3 egg yolks

9 tartlet tins, or bun pan

Method

Prepare the pastry and set aside to chill. Set oven at 375°F or Mark 5.

Boil the cream until reduced by one-third, stir in the béchamel sauce and, while still warm, beat in the cheese and then egg yolks. Leave to cool.

Roll out the pastry, cut into rounds and line the tins. Cut a lid for each one from remaining pastry. Spoon the filling into the pastry cases—they should be three-quarters full—and sit a lid on top of each one. Bake for about 20 minutes in pre-set oven until golden-brown. Serve hot.

Tartlets nicoise

For savoury shortcrust pastry
4 oz plain flour
salt and pepper
pinch of cayenne pepper
2 oz shortening
½ oz Parmesan cheese (grated)
½ egg yolk (mixed with 1
   tablespoon water)

For filling
2 oz curd, or cottage, cheese
½ oz butter
salt and pepper
4 black olives (finely chopped)

For garnish
1 hard-boiled egg

12-16 boat moulds

Method
Sift the flour with the seasonings, rub the shortening into the flour until mixture resembles fine breadcrumbs. Add cheese and mix to a dough with the egg yolk and water. Chill for 30 minutes. Set oven at 375°F or Mark 5.

Roll pastry out to ¼ inch thick and line into boat moulds. Line each pastry mould with a small piece of crumpled greaseproof paper and a few grains of rice, to hold the pastry in position. Bake for 7-8 minutes in the pre-set oven.

To prepare the filling: work the cheese with the butter until smooth, season and add the chopped olives. Fill this mixture into the baked pastry cases, doming it well and shaping it into an inverted V with a knife blade.

Arrange sieved egg yolk down one side and finely chopped egg white down the other.

Tartlets ricotta

For pastry
1 oz butter
2 oz lard
6 oz plain flour
pinch of salt
about 3 tablespoons water

For filling
10 oz curd cheese (home-made),
   or Demi-Sel
salt and pepper
3 eggs
2-3 oz smoked salmon, or ham
1-2 oz Gruyère cheese

12-16 tartlet tins, or 7-8 inch diameter flan ring

Method
Set oven at 375-400°F or Mark 5-6.

Rub the fats into the flour and salt and mix with the water to a firm dough.

To prepare filling: sieve and cream the curd cheese and add the seasoning. Beat the eggs and gradually add them to the cheese. Cut the salmon (or ham) into shreds and mix carefully into the egg and cheese mixture.

Roll out the pastry and line on to tartlet tins or flan ring. Fill with the prepared mixture. Cut the Gruyère cheese into thin slices and lay these over the top. Bake in the pre-set hot oven until golden-brown and crisp, about 12-15 minutes for tartlets, or about 25 minutes for a flan.

Roulades

·4 oz quantity savoury shortcrust
   pastry (see tartlets niçoise
   page 121)
French mustard
paprika pepper
Gentleman's Relish (Patum
   Pepperium)
1-2 tablespoons grated
   Parmesan cheese

Method

Roll out the shortcrust pastry
very thinly, to about ⅛ inch
thick, and spread thinly with
French mustard, dust with
paprika and then spread with a
little Gentleman's Relish and
sprinkle the cheese over the top.

Roll pastry up as for a swiss
roll, wrap in waxed or greaseproof paper and chill for 30
minutes. Cut the roll into ¼ inch
thick slices (or thinner if
possible) and place flat on a
baking sheet lined with greaseproof paper. Bake for about 8
minutes in a moderate oven,
pre-set at 375°F or Mark 5.

Savoury drop scones

4 oz plain flour
salt and pepper
pinch of cayenne pepper
1 teaspoon caster sugar
2 tablespoons grated Parmesan
   cheese
1 egg
2 tablespoons melted butter
¼ pint milk

These scones should be filled
at the last possible moment.
Following this recipe are three
suggested fillings. This quantity
will make about 24 scones.

Method

Heat a girdle or heavy frying
pan over moderate heat while
mixing the batter.

Sift the flour, seasonings and
sugar into the mixing bowl.
Add the Parmesan cheese and
mix well. Make a well in the
centre and drop in the egg and
melted butter, add the milk
gradually, beating well with a
wooden spoon. Grease the
girdle or frying pan very lightly
and pour the mixture from the
point of a spoon, or from a
jug, to give perfectly round,
small scones. As soon as the
'pancakes' are puffy and full of
bubbles and their undersides
golden-brown, lift them with a
palette knife, turn and brown
on the other side.

Serve immediately, or place
between the folds of a clean,
warm tea towel until ready to
serve. Do not reheat scones as
this would toughen them.

Filling 1

Remove rind and rust from rashers of finely cut streaky bacon. Stroke out rashers with blunt blade of a heavy knife until really thin. Cut rashers in half, spread with French mustard, roll up and skewer. These rolls can be grilled or baked, but they must be crisp and brown. They are best made with 'tender-sweet' streaky bacon and put into the scones while piping hot. Curl the scones around the bacon and secure with cocktail sticks.

Filling 2

2 oz cream cheese
salt and pepper
1 can (1¾ oz) Danish caviar
squeeze of lemon juice

Method

Season the cream cheese and spread on the hot scones.

Sprinkle the caviar well with the lemon juice and put ½ teaspoon of it in the centre of each scone. Fold over and secure with cocktail sticks.

Filling 3

For a really extravagant cocktail savoury put 1 teaspoon of pâté de foie gras on to each warm scone, and fold over. A less expensive way is to use liver pâté, carefully seasoned with a dash of French mustard and a few drops of brandy.

1 *Turning the savoury drop scones to brown each side*
2 *The scones are curled around bacon rolls and secured*

Marjolaine tartlets

For choux pastry
¼ pint water
2 oz butter
2½ oz plain flour
2 eggs
2 oz Cheddar cheese (grated)
salt and pepper

4 oz quantity rich shortcrust
  pastry

For cheese sauce
½ oz butter
1 tablespoon plain flour
½ pint milk (infused with 1 bayleaf, 1 slice of onion, 1 blade of
  mace, 6 peppercorns)
1½ oz cheese (grated)
salt and pepper

*6-8 tartlet tins; forcing bag and small
  round pipe*

Method
Line the tins with rich shortcrust pastry. Prick bottom of
pastry, line with greaseproof
paper and beans or rice and
bake blind for 10-15 minutes in
oven at 375°F or Mark 5.
  Prepare choux pastry (see
page 108). Pipe choux into
shortcrust pastry tartlets, leaving a hollow in the middle of
each one. Set oven at 400°F or
Mark 6.
  To prepare cheese sauce:
melt butter in a pan, stir in flour
and cook to a pale straw
colour. Strain milk, stir it on to
the roux and simmer for 2
minutes. Season and add
cheese to taste.
  Pour sauce into tartlets and
bake in pre-set oven for 15-20
minutes to cook choux pastry
gently, while browning the
cheese in the middle of the tartlets. Serve them immediately.

Cheese and sharp jelly canapés

For savoury almond pastry
4 oz plain flour
salt and pepper
pinch of cayenne pepper
2 oz shortening
½ oz almonds (blanched and
  ground)
½ egg yolk (mixed with 1 tablespoon water)

1 packet (2¾ oz) Demi-Sel, or
  cream cheese
1 oz butter
1 tablespoon hot milk (optional)
salt
piquant jelly (eg. redcurrant,
  quince, or grape)

*Plain cutter ($1\frac{1}{4}$ inches in diameter);
forcing bag and small rose pipe*

Method
Prepare pastry as for savoury
shortcrust (page 121), roll out
¼ inch thick and stamp into
rounds. Put on a baking sheet
lined with greaseproof paper
and bake for 7-8 minutes in an
oven pre-set at 375°F or Mark 5.
  Bind the cheese and butter
together, adding the hot milk,
if necessary, to thin the mixture
a little for piping; season to
taste with a little salt. Pipe the
cheese in a circle around the
edges of the canapés. Fill the
centres with a piquant jelly of
your choice.
Watchpoint To prevent the
jelly softening too much, cut it
from the jar with a salt spoon,
using the spoon as a scoop,
and insert it into the centre of
each canapé.

Cheese and smoked salmon canapés

4 oz quantity savoury almond
  shortcrust pastry (see left)
about 3 oz cream, or curd,
  cheese
salt and pepper
about 1 tablespoon hot milk
2 oz smoked salmon
black pepper (ground from mill)
squeeze of lemon juice

Forcing bag and vegetable rose pipe

Method

Roll out the almond pastry to ¼ inch thick and cut into oblongs 2 inches by 1 inch, then bake in a moderate oven, set at 375 °F or Mark 5, for 5-6 minutes.

Work the cream, or curd, cheese with seasoning and hot milk, to make a good consistency for piping. Put this into the forcing bag fitted with the vegetable rose pipe. Next chop the smoked salmon.

Watchpoint It is best to chop the salmon rather carefully with a serrated knife, cutting it first into thin strips and then crossways into very small dice. As smoked salmon is very oily, it tends to stick together if chopped in the usual way.

Season the salmon with black pepper and a little lemon juice. Pipe the cream cheese on the top of each canapé and sprinkle the top with the prepared smoked salmon.

Petites bouchées écossaises

4 oz quantity of puff pastry
1 egg (beaten)

For filling
1 packet (2¾ oz) Demi-Sel cheese
1 tablespoon double cream
3 oz smoked salmon (shredded)
black pepper (ground from mill)
squeeze of lemon juice

Fluted cutters (1½-inch and 1-inch diameter)

This quantity will make 8-9 small bouchées.

Method

Set oven at 425°F or Mark 7.

Roll out the puff pastry to no more than ¼ inch thick for these little bouchées.

Cut pastry into rounds or ovals with the larger fluted cutter. Set on a dampened baking sheet and brush with beaten egg. Mark a smaller circle in the centre of each bouchée for the lid. Chill for 10 minutes before baking in pre-set oven for 10-15 minutes.

To prepare the filling: beat the cheese until smooth, soften with the cream and add the shredded salmon; season with black pepper and lemon juice to taste.

When the bouchées are baked remove the tops and scoop away any soft pastry from the inside; allow to cool, then fill with the cheese and salmon mixture. Replace bouchée tops.

Ham and cream cheese rolls

½ lb cooked gammon (sliced)
2 packets (5½ oz) Demi-Sel
   cheese
1 tablespoon hot milk
salt and pepper
½ dill cucumber (chopped)
1 cap canned pimiento (chopped)
curled celery

Method

Cut each slice of ham in half.
Work the cream cheese with
the milk, season and add the
chopped dill cucumber and
pimiento. Put a spoonful of this
mixture on each piece of ham,
roll and fasten with a cocktail
stick. Serve garnished with
curled celery.

Stuffed avocado pears

3 avocado pears
1 packet (2-3 oz) cream cheese
1-2 teaspoons anchovy essence
6 black olives (chopped)
juice of 1 lemon
lettuce leaves (to garnish)
¼ pint vinaigrette dressing

Method

Work the cream cheese with the
anchovy essence and add the
chopped olives. Halve, skin
and remove the stones from the
avocados. Fill the cavities with
the cream cheese mixture and
re-shape. Roll each avocado
quickly in the lemon juice and
wrap in transparent self-clinging
wrapping paper or wet greaseproof paper to exclude the air.
Keep them refrigerated until
ready to serve.

Arrange crisp lettuce leaves
on a serving platter, slice the
avocados in rounds, place on
the lettuce and spoon over the
vinaigrette dressing.

Salt beef rolls

¼ lb salt beef brisket (thinly
   sliced)
2 oz curd, or cream, cheese
horseradish cream
few pickled walnuts

Method

Spread the slices of brisket with
cream cheese, flavoured with the
horseradish cream. Roll up and
fasten with cocktail sticks. Serve
garnished with pickled walnuts.

Stuffed grapes

1 lb large black grapes
4 oz cream cheese
salt
black pepper (to taste)
2 tablespoons finely chopped
 salted almonds

Method

Wipe the grapes and carefully take them off the stem. Split each one at the stalk end and carefully lift out the pips with the point of a knife.

Work the cream cheese with salt and black pepper to taste, put it into a cone of grease-proof paper and fill the grapes, allowing the cheese to come well above the top of each grape. Dip them into the salted almonds and serve on cocktail sticks or in small paper cases.

Savoury Danish ring

12 oz plain flour
large pinch of salt
1 oz yeast
1 oz caster sugar
7½ fl oz warm milk
9 oz butter
1 egg (beaten)

For filling
1 large onion (finely chopped)
2 oz butter
3 tablespoons breadcrumbs
salt and pepper
2 tablespoons ground almonds
2 tablespoons grated Parmesan
 cheese
½ beaten egg

To finish
½ beaten egg
1 tablespoon grated Parmesan
 cheese
1 tablespoon poppy, or sesame,
 seeds

Angel cake tin

Method

Sift the flour with the salt into a mixing bowl. Cream the yeast with the sugar until liquid. Add the warm milk and 2 oz of the butter and stir until dissolved; then add the beaten egg. Pour

Rolling up chilled dough before final proving

Savoury Danish ring continued

the liquid ingredients into the flour and mix to a smooth dough. Cover and leave at room temperature for about 1 hour, or until double in bulk.

Punch down the dough, turn it on to a floured board and knead lightly. Roll out to an oblong and cover two-thirds of the dough with half the remaining butter, divided in small pieces the size of a walnut, fold and roll as for flaky pastry. Fold in three and roll again. Put on remaining butter, fold and leave for 15 minutes. Roll and fold twice more, wrap in a clean tea towel and leave in the refrigerator for at least 15 minutes, but preferably 30 minutes, while preparing the filling.

For the filling: cook the onion in the butter until soft and golden, then add the bread-crumbs and season well. Tip into a bowl, work in the ground almonds and cheese and bind with a little beaten egg. Allow to cool.

Roll out the chilled dough to a large oblong, spread over the filling, roll up dough and join the ends to make a circle. Place in a very lightly buttered angel cake tin and prove in a warm place for 10-15 minutes, until well risen. Brush with beaten egg, dust with the Parmesan cheese and poppy or sesame seeds and bake for 45-50 minutes in a hot oven, pre-set at 400°F or Mark 6.

When cold, cut the ring into slices for serving.

Savoury Danish ring, dusted with cheese and poppy seeds

Camembert en surprise

1 ripe Camembert cheese
3 oz unsalted butter
3 tablespoons dried white
  breadcrumbs
3 tablespoons white wine
salt and pepper
1 bunch of radishes
4 black olives
3 tablespoons ground almonds
  (browned)
1 packet of pretzels

5-6 inch diameter sandwich tin

Method

Line the tin with a circle of greaseproof paper or foil.

Cut or scrape away the rind of Camembert and rub cheese through a wire strainer.

Cream butter until soft; add the cheese and work in the crumbs and wine, a little at a time. Season to taste. Put the mixture into the prepared tin, cover it with foil and chill for 2-3 hours.

Cut the radishes into roses and drop them in iced water; leave them for 1-2 hours to open. Halve the olives and remove the stones.

Before serving, turn out the cheese, roll it in the ground almonds, and press almonds into the top; lift carefully on to a serving dish. Mark the top in portions with the back of a knife and decorate with olives. Press pretzels round the cheese. Drain the radishes and arrange round the dish. Serve with thin water biscuits.

Camembert croquettes

1 Camembert cheese
1½ oz butter
1½ oz plain flour
½ pint milk
salt and pepper
pinch of cayenne pepper, or
  dash of Tabasco sauce
1 egg yolk
1 egg (beaten)
dry white breadcrumbs
2 tablespoons grated Parmesan
  cheese

Method

Scrape away the rind and press the cheese through a sieve. Melt the butter in a pan, blend in the flour and add the milk. Stir gently until boiling, season well and allow to cool.

Work the sieved cheese into the cold sauce, then add the egg yolk. Turn the mixture on to a plate and when it is absolutely cold shape it with a palette knife into pieces the size of a walnut. Dust with flour, brush with beaten egg and coat with crumbs. Fry in deep fat until golden-brown and dust with Parmesan cheese while still hot. Serve immediately.

Asparagus nordaise

1 bundle of asparagus
2 oz mushrooms
1¼ oz butter
salt and pepper
½ oz plain flour
5 fl oz top of milk
1½ oz cheese (grated)
hot buttered toast (for serving)

This quantity makes approximately 8 servings.

Method

Trim, cook and drain the asparagus. Wash and cut the mushrooms into thick slices, add to ¾ oz of the butter, melted, season and cook slowly with the pan lid on for 5-6 minutes.

Melt the remaining ½ oz butter in a pan, add the flour, mix together, then pour on the milk. Stir sauce until boiling; add the cheese and seasoning.

Arrange the mushrooms, and then 1-2 asparagus tips, on fingers of hot buttered toast. Spoon sauce over each one and glaze them under the grill.

Tomato and Gruyère toasts

3 tomatoes
3 oz Gruyère cheese (thinly sliced)
1 egg (lightly beaten)
¼ pint milk
salt and pepper
3 slices of white bread
2 oz butter
1 teaspoon French mustard
(preferably Dijon mustard)
salt and pepper
1 sprig of rosemary

Method

Mix together the egg, milk, salt and pepper. Remove the crusts from the bread, cut each slice into three and soak in the egg and milk.

Meanwhile heat the butter in a frying pan, then fry the bread slowly so that a crust is formed at the bottom before the bread is turned and browned on the other side. Spread the fried bread very thinly with a good French mustard. Put in a warm shallow casserole ready for grilling and place the slices of Gruyère cheese on top.

Scald and skin the tomatoes, cut the core from the top, squeeze gently to remove some of the seeds, then cut them in thick slices and arrange on top of the cheese. Season lightly and dust with sugar; spike the slices with a few leaves of rosemary. Put a tiny knob of butter on each tomato slice and grill until the cheese bubbles and begins to brown. Serve hot.

1 *Frying the pieces of soaked bread in the butter until crusty and golden-brown*
2 *Season the toasts before grilling, and put a knob of butter on each tomato slice*

Tomato and Gruyère toasts continued

Savoury tomato and Gruyère toasts, garnished with rosemary

Appendix

Notes and basic recipes

Almonds

Buy them with their skins on. This way they retain their oil better. Blanching to remove the skins gives extra juiciness.

To blanch: pour boiling water over the shelled nuts, cover the pan and leave until cool. Then the skins can be easily removed (test one with finger and thumb). Drain, rinse in cold water, press skins off with fingers. Rinse, dry thoroughly.

To brown almonds: blanch and bake for 7-8 minutes in a moderate oven at 350°F or Mark 4.

To chop almonds: first blanch, skin, chop and then brown them in the oven, if desired.

To shred almonds: first blanch, skin, split in two and cut each half lengthways in fine pieces. These can then be used as they are or browned quickly in the oven, with or without a sprinkling of caster sugar.

To flake almonds: first blanch, skin, and cut horizontally into flakes with a small sharp knife.

To grind almonds: first blanch, skin, chop and pound into a paste (use a pestle and mortar, or a grinder, or the butt end of a rolling pin). Home-prepared ground almonds taste much better than the ready ground variety.

Aspic jelly

2½ fl oz sherry
2½ fl oz white wine
2 oz gelatine
1¾ pints cold stock
1 teaspoon wine vinegar
2 egg whites

Method
Add wines to gelatine and set aside. Pour cold stock into scalded pan, add vinegar. Whisk egg whites to a froth, add them to the pan, set over moderate heat and whisk backwards and downwards (the reverse of the usual whisking movement) until the stock is hot.

Then add gelatine, which by now will have absorbed the wine, and continue whisking steadily until boiling point is reached.

Stop whisking and allow liquid to rise to the top of the pan; turn off heat or draw pan aside and leave to settle for about 5 minutes, then bring it again to the boil, draw pan aside once more and leave liquid to settle. At this point the liquid should look clear; if not, repeat the boiling-up process.

Filter the jelly through a scalded cloth or jelly bag.

The aspic should be allowed to cool before use.

The stock for aspic jelly may be white (chicken or veal), brown (beef) or fish, according to the dish being made.

Béchamel sauce

¾ pint milk
slice of onion
6 peppercorns
1 blade of mace
1 bayleaf
1 tablespoon cream (optional)

For roux
1 oz butter
2 tablespoons plain flour
salt and pepper

Method
Infuse milk with onion and spices in a covered pan over a low heat for 5-7 minutes, but do not boil. Pour the milk into a basin and wipe the pan out.

To make the roux: melt the butter slowly, remove pan from heat and stir in the flour. Pour on at least one-third of the milk through a strainer and blend together with a wooden spoon. Then add the rest of the milk, season lightly, return to heat and stir until boiling. Boil for not more than 2 minutes, then taste for seasoning. The sauce may be finished with 1 tablespoon of cream.

Breadcrumbs

To make white crumbs: take a large loaf (the best type to use is a sandwich loaf) at least two days old. Cut off the crust and keep to one side. Break up bread into crumbs either by rubbing through a wire sieve or a Mouli sieve, or by working in an electric blender.

To dry crumbs: spread crumbs on a sheet of paper laid on a baking tin and cover with another sheet of paper to keep off any dust. Leave to dry in a warm temperature — the plate rack, or warming drawer, or the top of the oven, or even the airing cupboard, is ideal. The crumbs may take a day or two to dry thoroughly, and they must be crisp before storing in a jar. To make them uniformly fine, sift them through a wire bowl strainer.

To make browned crumbs: bake the crusts in a slow oven until golden-brown, then crush or grind through a mincer. Sift and store as for white crumbs. These browned ones are known as raspings and are used for any dish that is coated with a sauce and browned in the oven.

Mayonnaise

2 egg yolks
salt and pepper
dry mustard
¾ cup salad oil
2 tablespoons wine vinegar

This recipe will make ½ pint of mayonnaise.

Method

Work egg yolks and seasonings with a small whisk or wooden spoon in a bowl until thick; then start adding the oil drop by drop. When 2 tablespoons of oil have been added this mixture will be very thick. Now carefully stir in 1 teaspoon of the vinegar.

The remaining oil can then be added a little more quickly, either 1 tablespoon at a time and beaten thoroughly between each addition until it is absorbed, or in a thin steady stream if you are using an electric beater.

When all the oil has been absorbed, add remaining vinegar to taste, and extra salt and pepper as necessary.

To thin and lighten mayonnaise, add a little hot water. For a coating consistency, thin with a little cream or milk.

Eggs should not come straight from the refrigerator. If oil is cloudy or chilled, it can be slightly warmed which will lessen the chances of eggs curdling. Put oil bottle in a pan of hot water for a short time.

Watchpoint Great care must be taken to prevent mayonnaise curdling. Add oil drop by drop at first, and then continue adding it very slowly.

If mayonnaise curdles, start with a fresh yolk in another bowl and work well with seasoning, then add the curdled mixture to it very slowly and carefully. When curdled mixture is completely incorporated, more oil can be added if the mixture is too thin.

Pastry

Choux pastry

¼ pint (5 fl oz) water
2 oz butter, or margarine
2½ oz plain flour
2 eggs

Method

Put water and fat into a fairly large pan. Sift flour on to a piece of paper. Bring contents of the pan to the boil and when bubbling draw pan aside, allow bubbles to subside and pour in all the flour at once. Stir vigorously until it is smooth (a few seconds).

Cool mixture for about 5 minutes, then beat in the eggs one at a time.

▶ 135

If eggs are large, break the last one into a bowl and beat with a fork. Add this slowly to ensure that the mixture remains firm and keeps its shape (you may not need to use all of this last egg).

Beat pastry for about 3 minutes until it looks glossy. It is then ready to be piped out, using a plain éclair pipe, or shaped with a spoon for baking or frying.

French flan pastry

4 oz plain flour
pinch of salt
2 oz butter
2 oz caster sugar
2-3 drops of vanilla essence
2 egg yolks

Method
Sieve the flour with a pinch of salt on to a marble slab or pastry board, make a well in the centre and in it place the butter, sugar, vanilla essence and egg yolks. Using the fingertips of one hand only, pinch and work these last three ingredients together until well blended. Then draw in the flour, knead lightly until smooth.

Puff pastry

8 oz plain flour
pinch of salt
8 oz butter
1 teaspoon lemon juice
scant ¼ pint water (ice cold)

Method
Sift flour and salt into a bowl. Rub in a piece of butter the size of a walnut. Add lemon juice to water, make a well in centre of flour and pour in about two-thirds of the liquid. Mix with a palette, or round-bladed, knife. When the dough is beginning to form, add remaining water.

Turn out the dough on to a marble slab, a laminated-plastic work top,
or a board, dusted with flour. Knead dough for 2-3 minutes, then roll out to a square about ½-¾ inch thick.

Beat butter, if necessary, to make it pliable and place in centre of dough. Fold this up over butter to enclose it completely (sides and ends over centre like a parcel). Wrap in a cloth or piece of grease-proof paper and put in the refrigerator for 10-15 minutes.

Flour slab or work top, put on dough, the join facing upwards, and bring rolling pin down on to dough 3-4 times to flatten it slightly.

Now roll out to a rectangle about ½-¾ inch thick. Fold into three, ends to middle, as accurately as possible, if necessary pulling the ends to keep them rectangular. Seal the edges with your hand or rolling pin and turn pastry half round to bring the edge towards you. Roll out again and fold in three (keep a note of the 'turns' given). Set pastry aside in refrigerator for 15 minutes. Repeat this process twice, giving a total of 6 turns with a 15 minute rest after each two turns. Then leave in the refrigerator until wanted.

Rich shortcrust pastry

8 oz plain flour
pinch of salt
6 oz butter
1 rounded dessertspoon caster
sugar (for sweet pastry)
1 egg yolk
2-3 tablespoons cold water

Method
Sift the flour with a pinch of salt into a mixing bowl. Drop in the butter and cut it into the flour until the small pieces are well coated. Then rub them in with the fingertips until the mixture looks like fine breadcrumbs. Stir in the sugar, mix egg yolk with water, tip into the fat and flour and mix quickly with a palette knife to a firm dough.

Turn on to a floured board and knead lightly until smooth. If possible, chill in refrigerator (wrapped in greaseproof paper, a polythene bag or foil) for 30 minutes before using.

Rough puff pastry

8 oz plain flour
pinch of salt
6 oz firm butter, or margarine
¼ pint ice-cold water (to mix)

Method
Sift the flour with salt into a mixing bowl. Cut the fat in even-size pieces about the size of walnuts and drop into the flour. Mix quickly with the water (to prevent overworking dough so that it becomes starchy) and turn on to a lightly-floured board.

Complete the following action three times: roll to an oblong, fold in three and make a half-turn to bring the open edges in front of you so that the pastry has three turns in all. Chill for 10 minutes and give an extra roll and fold if it looks at all streaky, then use as required.

Shortcrust pastry

8 oz plain flour
pinch of salt
4-6 oz butter, margarine, lard or shortening (one of the commercially prepared fats), or a mixture of any two
3-4 tablespoons cold water

Method
Sift the flour with a pinch of salt into a mixing bowl. Cut the fat into the flour with a round-bladed knife and, as soon as the pieces are well coated with flour, rub in with the fingertips until the mixture looks like fine breadcrumbs.

Make a well in the centre, add the water (reserving about 1 tablespoon) and mix quickly with a knife. Press together with the fingers, adding the extra water, if necessary, to give a firm dough.

Turn on to a floured board, knead pastry lightly until smooth. Chill in refrigerator (wrapped in grease-proof paper, a polythene bag or foil) for 30 minutes before using.

To bake blind Chill pastry case, line with crumpled greaseproof paper and three-parts fill with uncooked rice or beans. An 8-inch diameter flan ring holding a 6-8 oz quantity of pastry should cook for about 26 minutes in an oven at 400°F or Mark 6. Take out paper and beans for last 5 minutes baking.

Stocks

Bouillon

3 lb rolled rib of beef (with the bones)
1 lb knuckle of veal, or a veal bone
1 dessertspoon salt
about 5 pints water
2 large carrots (quartered)
2-3 onions (one stuck with a clove)
2-3 sticks of celery
1-2 turnips (quartered)
large bouquet garni

This recipe is for making both a classic French bouillon and the French version of boiled beef at the same time. The beef is un-salted and is gently simmered with root vegetables for 2-3 hours. When the beef is tender it is taken out with the vegetables and served as the main course.

Method
Put the meat into a large pan with the salted water and the washed bones of both the beef and veal. Put on a slow heat without a lid and bring to the boil. As the scum rises to the surface, take it off with a metal spoon and, as the liquid reaches simmering point, add about a coffee cup (2½ fl oz) of cold water.

137

Bring to the boil again, skim once more and add a further coffee cup of cold water. If the liquid is still not clear, this process can be repeated once more. This procedure is not only to help clear the liquid, which will become soup, but also to remove any strong flavour of bone. Simmer for about 30-40 minutes, then add the vegetables and the bouquet garni. Continue to simmer, skimming again if necessary, and partially cover the pan with the lid. Simmer until the meat is tender (approximately 2½-3 hours), then remove the meat and serve it with the vegetables.

Return the pan to the heat and continue to simmer until bouillon is strong and well flavoured to use for soups.

Brown bone stock

3 lb beef bones (or mixed beef/veal)
2 onions (quartered)
2 carrots (quartered)
1 stick of celery
large bouquet garni
6 peppercorns
3-4 quarts water
salt

6-quart capacity saucepan, or small fish kettle

Method
Wipe bones but do not wash unless unavoidable. Put into a very large pan. Set on gentle heat and leave bones to fry gently for 15-20 minutes. Enough fat will come out from the marrow so do not add any to pan unless bones are very dry.

After 10 minutes add the vegetables, having sliced the celery into 3-4 pieces.

When bones and vegetables are just coloured, add herbs, peppercorns, salt and water, which should come up two-thirds above level of ingredients. Bring slowly to the boil, skimming occasionally, then half cover pan to allow reduction to take

place and simmer 4-5 hours, or until stock tastes strong and good.

Strain off and use bones again for a second boiling. Although this second stock will not be so strong as the first, it is good for soups and gravies. Use the first stock for brown sauces, sautées, casseroles, or where a jellied stock is required. For a strong beef broth, add 1 lb shin of beef to the pot halfway through the cooking.

Chicken stock
This should ideally be made from the giblets (neck, gizzard, heart and feet, if available), but never the liver which imparts a bitter flavour. This is better kept for making pâté, or sautéed and used as a savoury. Dry fry the giblets with an onion, washed but not peeled, and cut in half. To dry fry, use a thick pan with a lid, with barely enough fat to cover the bottom. Allow the pan to get very hot before putting in the giblets and onion, cook on full heat until lightly coloured. Remove pan from heat before covering with 2 pints of cold water. Add a large pinch of salt, a few peppercorns and a bouquet garni (bay leaf, thyme, parsley) and simmer gently for 1-2 hours. Alternatively, make the stock when you cook the chicken by putting the giblets in the roasting tin around the chicken with the onion and herbs, and use the measured quantity of water.

Vegetable stock

1 lb carrots (quartered)
1 lb onions (quartered)
½ head of celery (sliced)
½ oz butter
3-4 peppercorns
1 teaspoon tomato purée
2 quarts water
salt

Method
Quarter vegetables, brown lightly in the butter in a large pan. Add

peppercorns, tomato purée, water and salt. Bring to boil, cover pan and simmer 2 hours or until the stock has a good flavour.

Tomatoes

To skin tomatoes: place them in a bowl, scald by pouring boiling water over them, count 12, then pour off the hot water and replace it with cold. The skin then comes off easily.

To remove seeds: slice off the top of each tomato and flick out seeds with the handle of a teaspoon, use bowl of spoon to detach core.

White sauce

¾ oz butter
1 rounded tablespoon plain flour
½ pint milk
salt and pepper

Method
Melt the butter in a small pan, remove from heat and stir in the flour. Blend in half the milk, then stir in the rest. Stir this over moderate heat until boiling, then boil gently for 1-2 minutes. Season to taste.

Glossary

Bain-marie (au) To cook at temperature just below boiling point in a bain-marie (a saucepan standing in a larger pan of simmering water). Used in the preparation of sauces, creams and food liable to spoil if cooked over direct heat. May be carried out in oven or on top of stove. A double saucepan gives similar result. Sauces and other delicate dishes may be kept hot in a bain-marie at less than simmering heats.

Blanch To whiten meats and remove strong tastes from vegetables by bringing to boil from cold water and draining before further cooking. Green vegetables should be put into boiling water and cooked for up to 1 minute.

Bouquet garni Traditionally a bunch of parsley, thyme, bayleaf, for flavouring stews and sauces. Other herbs can be added. Remove before serving dish.

Butter, clarified Butter clarified by heating gently until foaming, skimming well, pouring off clear yellow oil, leaving sediment (milk solids) behind.

Croûte Small round of bread, lightly toasted or fried, spread or piled up with a savoury mixture, also used as a garnish. Not to be confused with pie or bread crust (also croûte).

Croûton Small square or dice of fried bread or potato to accompany purée or cream soups.

Dégorger To remove impurities and strong flavours before cooking by:
1 Soaking food, eg. uncooked ham, in cold water for specified length of time. 2 Sprinkling sliced vegetables, eg. cucumber, with salt, covering with heavy plate, leaving up to 1 hour, and pressing out excess liquid with a weighted plate.

Gratin (au) Strictly, to cook dish covered in crumbs, butter, sauce, grated cheese in oven. Term sometimes used for browning cooked dish under grill.

Infuse To steep in liquid (not always boiling) in warm place to draw flavour into the liquid.

Poussin Baby chicken (4-6 weeks old), usually sufficient for only one person. Double poussins (6-10 weeks old) are slightly larger and will serve two.

Roux Fat and flour liaison. This is the basis of all flour sauces. The weight of fat should generally be slightly more than that of flour. To make, melt fat, stir in flour (off heat) and pour on water/stock/milk. Stir until roux thickens, bring to boil and cook.

Sauté To brown food in butter or oil and butter. Sometimes cooking is completed in a 'small' sauce — ie. one made on the food in the sauté pan.

Shortening Fat which when worked into flour gives a short crisp quality to pastry/cakes. Fats with least liquid, eg. lard, vegetable fat, contain most shortening power.

Index